ANGELS NOBLES & UNICORNS

ART AND PATRONAGE IN MEDIEVAL SCOTLAND

A handbook published in conjunction with an
exhibition held at the National Museum of Scotland
August 12–September 26, 1982

NATIONAL MUSEUM OF ANTIQUITIES OF SCOTLAND
EDINBURGH
1982

Printed in Scotland for HMSO by Buccleuch Printers Ltd, Hawick.

ISBN 0 9503117 1 5

CONTENTS

PREFACE

This booklet, produced under considerable difficulties because of current restrictions on finance and on staff, is intended to present a basic, illustrated guide to the productions of the higher levels of culture in medieval Scotland, from about 1100 to 1550. It is based on the contents of an exhibition, *Angels, Nobles and Unicorns,* mounted in the National Museum's new extension in York Buildings, from 12 August till 26 September 1982. In the first instance it sets out to show the considerable range of material held by the National Museum itself, a historical and artistic resource that is of the utmost importance for the material culture of Scotland at a period about which we have little writing on that topic. It also rounds up a large number of items that were dispersed outside Scotland, at and after the Reformation. The material, which includes examples of sculptures, illustrated manuscripts and objects produced in or for Scotland under royal, church and lay patronage, covers the period of the foundation of the monasteries and the development of their architecture and sculpture. Many items not seen in Scotland since the 16th century are brought together, and the result is a degree of considerable astonishment at the wealth and artistic level of this small country at that remote period. This list illustrates that wealth. We offer it, not as a definitive work of scholarship, but as a base which scholars may use in their more specialised work, and as a source of interest and pleasure for their readers.

A word should be said about the origins of the exhibition. In 1975, Malcolm Baker, formerly of the Royal Scottish Museum, Richard Emerson, formerly of the National Monuments Record, and John Higgitt of the Department of Fine Art of Edinburgh University, conceived the idea of a display on the Romanesque and early Gothic art in Scotland between the 11th and 13th centuries, under the central theme of Scottish royal patronage from the time of Queen Margaret onwards. In 1977, the National Museum of Antiques became involved, mainly because so much of the relevant material is in its collections. The period was also extended by a couple of centuries to allow for greater variety of exhibits.

In the development of thinking that has led to the exhibition, the National Museum is under a great debt of gratitude to a group of people whose knowledge comprises the bulk of what is presently known about the material culture of medieval Scotland. They are:-

Malcolm Baker, formerly Royal Scottish Museum

Dr David H Caldwell, National Museum of Antiquities of Scotland

Richard Emerson, formerly National Monuments Record

Dr Richard Fawcett, Scottish Development Department (Ancient Monuments Division)

Dr Tessa Garton, Department of History of Fine Art, University of Aberdeen

John Higgitt, Department of Fine Art, University of Edinburgh

Geoffrey Stell, Royal Commission on the Ancient and Historical Monuments of Scotland

Elspeth Yeo, National Library of Scotland.

We appreciate in particular the forbearance of John Higgitt. Information on manuscripts with a Scottish medieval provenance, from the text of his lecture to the Society of Antiquaries of Scotland in Spring 1980 and from his unpublished handlist of decorated books in medieval Scotland, has been made use of in this list. He takes no responsibility for the form in which this information has been used.

Without the help of such people, the exhibition and this list, would be much poorer or might have been impossible to produce.

Alexander Fenton
Director

ACKNOWLEDGEMENTS

The Board of Trustees and the Staff of the National Museum of Antiquities of Scotland acknowledge with gratitude the generous support of the following:
  Bank of Scotland
  The Royal Bank of Scotland plc
  Clydesdale Bank PLC
  The Dulverton Trust
  The Scottish International Education Trust
  Scottish and Newcastle Breweries Limited
  The Cruden Foundation Limited
  The Russell Trust
They are also indebted to Tullis Russell & Co Ltd for the supply of paper.

The bulk of the entries in this booklet have been prepared by Elizabeth Sharratt, with contributions from others, including Andrea Gilbert, Ruth Summers, Kathryn Morrison and Jennifer Blakebell, all working either as volunteers or temporary assistants.
  The whole has been edited by Dr D H Caldwell.

PHOTOGRAPHS

All the illustrations are the work of Ian Larner and Doreen Moyes of the National Museum of Antiquities of Scotland's photographic department, except the following:
  Aberdeen University Library: E58
  Bodleian Library, Oxford: B16
  British Library: C27, E59
  British Museum: B27, B34, C30, C51, C54, C58, D15, E71, E81, E103, E104
  The Master and Fellows of Corpus Christi College, Cambridge: E42
  Courtald Institute of Art: E39, E61
  Edinburgh University Library: A2, E28, E60, E63
  Glasgow Art Gallery and Museums: B29, B32, E12
  Godfrey New Photographics Ltd: C17
  National Library of Scotland: B19, B22, C21, C24, C26, E40
  Public Record Office, London: E33
  St Andrews University Library: E48
  Tom Scott & J McLeod of McLeod: D11
  Verulamium Museum, St Albans: F22
  Victoria and Albert Museum: B25, B41

INTRODUCTION

The art of a country is like a mirror reflecting the essence of its life. This is particularly true of Scotland in the Middle Ages where two effects of major political events like the influx of a new ruling class in the 12th and war with England at the end of the 13th centuries were the swamping of native art by the more acceptable international Romanesque and a turning away from English example both inwards and to the Continent.

The clear division of Scotland by the 14th century into two cultures speaking two different languages, Gaelic and Scots, is also recognisable, with the distinctive art of the West Highlands and the Lowland 'mainstream', largely based on the burghs as centres of craftsmanship.

Owing to our imperfect knowledge of the period it is often difficult to distinguish between the works of Scottish artists and craftsmen and foreign imports, though this in itself may say much about Scottish taste. We should not assume, as has often been done in the past, that where there is doubt about whether to attribute, say, a piece of woodcarving to a Flemish or Scottish workshop, that poor quality makes the latter more likely. In some ways it matters not whether the silver gilt print in the Bute Mazer is Scottish or Continental work of the early 14th century. What is important is what this representation of King Robert Bruce as a lion surrounded by the enamelled shields of his leading nobles tells us about the pride of a victorious people, about national vitality.

Finally we come to the people who were the patrons of art in Scotland. Inevitably the story relates largely to the tastes of the Scottish kings, the nobles and the Church. Enough remains of the great churches built through the generosity of kings and nobles and the illuminated books commissioned by church-men to evoke an image of a society which appreciated the finer things in life.

The role of the merchants and craftsmen in the burghs and even the lesser country folk should not, however, be underestimated. A high quality of life was enjoyed by the better off burgesses who not only had richly decorated clothes, accessories and utensils but lavished money and attention, sometimes individually, sometimes as members of guilds and crafts, on the decoration of their burgh churches.

All this made for an art which was as diverse as it was colourful and rich. At times it may seem homely, staid or conservative, but it also encompasses the exuberance of Melrose Abbey and the excesses of Roslin Collegiate Church, the intricacies of saintly relics and the magnificence of a royal crown. It was cut short in the upheavals of the 16th century, making way for a remarkable expression of national consciousness in an art infused with the motifs of Renaissance Europe.

Brechin Cathedral with its 11th century round tower

1 THE ART OF THE EARLY SCOTTISH KINGDOM

The land which is now Scotland was formerly divided amongst several peoples. In the West Highlands and Islands was the Scottish kingdom of Dalriada, whose inhabitants maintained strong links with their kinsmen in Ireland. In the East was the kingdom of the Picts. South of the Forth the Lothians had been settled by English people and formed a northern extension of the kingdom of Bernicia. In the 9th century the northern and western parts were occupied by Scandinavian people who also settled further south in England, cutting Scotland off from contacts with Ireland and the rest of Britain. But far from being submerged politically and culturally by the Norse settlers the peoples of Scotland came to be united under a new and powerful Scottish line of kings, starting with Kenneth MacAlpin who in about 843 united the kingdoms of the Scots and the Picts. His descendants extended their rule to include Strathclyde in the south-west and Lothian as far south as the Tweed in the east.

About 1068, Malcolm III (Canmore), married an English princess, Margaret, and it is from about this time, at first tentatively, that Scotland began to absorb the art and culture of England, France and the countries beyond. These links came to be a dominant force in the succeeding centuries, though Scotland was able to develop its own variants of Romanesque and Gothic Art.

Very little in the way of art can be associated with this newly emergent kingdom in the years prior to 1068. The lively tradition of Pictish art, particularly in stone carving, came to an end in the 9th century and there seems to be little to bridge the gap between it and the Romanesque art of the 12th century. A few pieces of early workmanship like the 8th century Pictish *Monymusk Reliquary* continued to be of importance, indeed right through the Medieval Period, in this case owing to its associations with St Columba. Irish art continued to be transmitted to Scotland thanks largely to the shared traditions of the Celtic Church in both countries. The round tower at the important ecclesiastical centre of Brechin, an outstanding exception to a general lack of stone architecture in this period, like a similar tower at Abernethy, betrays Irish influence. It is unclear whether items of metalwork like the crozier of St Fillan or manuscripts like the *Book of Deer* and the *Celtic Psalter* are Irish or Scottish, but there is a small group of metalwork, including St Fillan's bell and some swivel rings with animal head terminals which seem to be peculiarly Scottish.

Perhaps if Scotland had remained isolated from contacts with the outside world its native tradition would have developed and flourished on its own but in the event it was submerged, though not totally, by the incoming Romanesque and Gothic forms in the Lowlands. In the Western Isles and Highlands elements of native art had a remarkable persistence, even enjoying a renaissance in the 16th century.

A1 Cross fragment

Northumbrian 9th century
110×270×210 mm
from Lasswade, Midlothian
Edinburgh, National Museum IB 21

The right arm of a free armed cross of Northumbrian type. It is carved on one side with a lion with long curling tongue and tail tucked between its legs. Stylistically it compares with representations of animals in manuscripts and on metalwork of the ninth century from Central England.

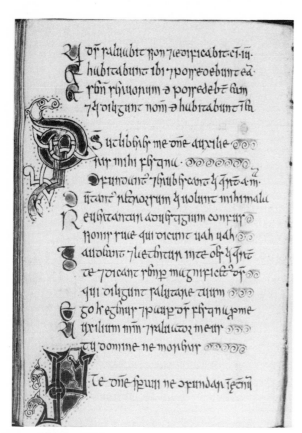

A2   Celtic Psalter

3   Psalm 118 (119) and prayers

Scotland Late 15th–Early 16th century
175×300 mm
Edinburgh, National Library of Scotland Advocates
72.1.4

The manuscript also contains medical texts and
notes in Gaelic as well as Latin. The script is Gaelic.
The writing preserves a late example of the Insular
script of the eleventh-century Celtic Psalter (E.U.L
56). The manuscript is decorated with touches of red
on the initials.

A4   The Monymusk reliquary

Scotland Early 8th century
112×51×89 mm
The reliquary is thought to be the Brecbennoch of St
Columba which was granted by William The Lion to
the Monks of Arbroath with the lands of Forglen
before 1211. In 1314 Bernard, Abbot of Arbroath,
gave the reliquary and its lands to Malcolm of
Monymusk. It remained from then on in
Monymusk in the possession of the family owning
the castle there.
Edinburgh, National Museum KE 14

The reliquary is in the form of a house-shrine and is
similar to a few Irish examples dating to the eighth
and ninth centuries. The decoration of this one,
particularly the work on the front plate, marks it as
an example of Pictish metalwork. It consists of a box
and a lid in the form of a hipped roof, each hollowed
out of a single piece of wood. It has been fitted with
bronze and silver plates lightly incised with
interlaced animal decoration and a series of round
and oblong plaques, two of which are missing. The
one surviving strap hinge is decorated with enamel
and the round bar forming the roof ridge is set with
blue glass beads in the terminals and a central plaque
with interlaced gold wire.

The purpose of such a reliquary is not certain. It is
possible that it was originally used to contain some
bones of the Saint. Another interpretation is that it
was used to carry round the Eucharist and holy oil for
the sick, hence the fittings for a neck strap.

PSAS, lxviii (1933–4), 433–8

A5   Four bronze ornaments including two 'swivel' rings

Scotland 11th century
Found in A'Chrois on Tiree, Valvay and Inver-
keithing respectively. Locality of FC 127 unknown.
Edinburgh, National Museum FC 266/267/128/127

These four ornaments are decorated in the ring part

A2   Psalter

Scotland or Ireland 11th century
160×240 mm
Edinburgh, University Library no 56

This psalter may have belonged to Queen Margaret
(d. 1093), the English wife of Malcolm III. It is a
pocket psalter written in Irish minuscule script and
decorated with a type of ornament also found in Irish
manuscripts deriving from the Hiberno-Saxon style
of the seventh and eighth centuries. The psalm
initials are formed of stylized animal figures with
bodies of interlaced black or coloured bands. In
addition, the initial letters of the verses on each page
are coloured in with purple, green, blue, yellow or
red. Of the original three full page decorations, only
one has survived (folio 50 r), preceding psalm 51. It
has been repainted in a late Anglo-Saxon style.

Borland, *Western Medieval MSS*, 100–102;
McRoberts, *Scottish Medieval Liturgical Books*, no 4.

with two snake-like animal heads facing one another. On the 'Swivel' rings these animal heads grasp the hoop which in both cases has lost its rivet. A similar application of the device is found on other early Scottish ornaments such as brooches and buckles. The handles of the St Fillan's Bell and the Kilmichael Glassary Bell Shrine are decorated at the terminals with comparable animal heads.

PSAS, cv (1972–4), 189ff; *Archaeol Journ*, cxxiii (1976), 280

A6 St Fillan's bell

Scotland 12th century
0.29×0.22×0.17 m
Said to have lain on a grave stone in the old churchyard of Strathfillan in Perthshire where it was used as a magical cure for various diseases until 1798 when it was removed and taken to England. It was returned to Scotland in 1869.
Edinburgh, National Museum KA 2

A cast bronze quadrangular hand-bell with an out-turned lip and a handle which is unusually decorated with animal-head terminals. Inside there is a loop for hanging a clapper. The bell resembles, in shape and size, a number of other hand bells surviving in Scotland, some made of sheet iron, others cast of bronze, which are thought to date to the ninth century. The out-turned lip of the St Fillan's bell and its tall, narrowing profile, however, indicate a twelfth-century date.

PSAS, viii (1868–70), 265–76

A4 The Monymusk reliquary

A7 St Fillan's crozier

Scotland or Ireland 11th century
155×160 mm
Kept at Eyich near Crianlarich for a number of centuries by the hereditory guardians of the shrine, the Dewars of Glendochart.
Edinburgh, National Museum KC 3

The bronze crook formed the early shrine of the supposed pastoral staff of St Fillan of Glendochart. It was discovered enclosed within the later shrine of the staff. It is composed of two bronze parts decorated with bands of metal in relief, formerly inlaid with niello, which divide the surface of the crook into lozenge shaped spaces. These were filled with plaques of filigree work some of which were transferred to the second case.

The shrine resembles a type of early medieval Irish crozier and staff shrine of which several have survived. The St Tola's crozier from the monastery of Dysert O'Dea, County Clare has a similar sort of decoration.

PSAS, xliv (1909–10), 279

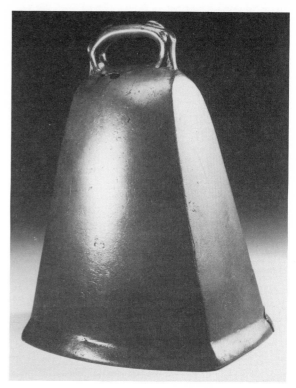

A6   St Fillan's Bell

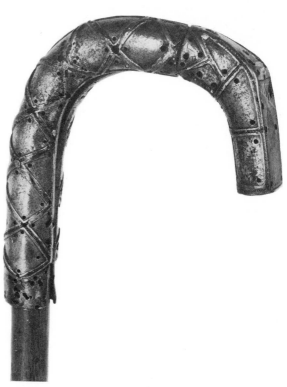

2 NEW BEGINNINGS

During the 12th century Scotland developed into a stable and increasingly powerful kingdom under the leadership of Malcolm III's successors. Basic to this transformation was the infiltration of Anglo-Norman culture into Scotland through contacts with England, a process which was accelerated by the policies of David I (1124–53) who had been brought up at the English court and who was one of the greatest land-holders in England. David imposed Norman methods of organisation and administration on his kingdom and encouraged the settlement of members of Anglo-Norman families, Flemings and others. To some he gave vast tracts of land and they in turn subinfeudated parcels of it to their own followers. David reorganised the Scottish church, bringing it more into line with the church in England and the Continent, and favoured foreigners were given positions of importance in it. David's reign also saw the birth of the burghs in Scotland, like Berwick, Edinburgh and Perth, which became prosperous trading centres, attracting merchants and craftsmen from outside Scotland.

King David's policies were followed and built upon by his successors, Malcolm IV (1153–65) and William I (1165–1214), thus ensuring that Scottish art and culture were exposed to Anglo-Norman tradition over a long period of time.

The strongest reflection of the new impetus in Scottish art in this century is found in ecclesiastical architecture. As a result of royal policy the number and variety of religious foundations was increased on an unprecedented scale. David, continuing the reform and expansion of the church that was begun by his mother Queen Margaret, was personally responsible for instituting several monastic houses including Melrose, Holyrood, Cambuskenneth, Jedburgh and Kelso. Others were founded by his immediate successors and the greater nobles, for example the FizAlans (Stewarts), the de Morvilles and the Lords of Galloway. At no other time in Scotland was so much money and effort expended on the glorification of the church by the ruling classes, and the evidence of this can be seen in the surviving architecture and furnishings of the monasteries

before the Wars of Independence.

Scottish ecclesiastical architecture looked to the innovations of English Romanesque and Gothic. The Romanesque style, which became established in Scotland by the middle of the twelfth century, was closely modelled on the English. The small churches at Tyninghame, Dalmeny and Leuchars follow the plan and decorative treatment of the simplest type of English Romanesque church, and the magnificent nave of Dunfermline Abbey which was commenced *c.* 1128 was directly influenced by the nave of Durham Cathedral. The buildings of the period, however, were not merely imitations of English examples. Even at this stage there was a tendency to produce individual idiomatic forms. The Abbeys of Jedburgh and Kelso, for example, monuments of a transitional phase between Romanesque and Gothic in Scottish architecture, have strongly individual characters. Jedburgh's early choir of which two bays survive has an original interpretation of Romanesque arcading with the first storey formed of massive drum piers divided into two levels of arcade. The well-proportioned west front with the Romanesque doorway and a rose window is an accomplishment in its own terms.

The 12th century parish church of Dalmeny, near Edinburgh – the tower is a recent rebuilding

Dalmeny Church, interior, looking into the apse

Dalmeny Church, south door

Kelso also must have had an impressive and original west front with a doorway similar to that on the existing north transept.

In other areas of artistic activity Scotland succumbed completely to English and continental influences. As with architecture, so with manuscripts. Irish tendencies were replaced by the Romanesque style, the only known exception to this being the 'Coupar Angus' Psalter which may in fact be Irish. During the spread of monasticism in Scotland in the 12th century most book decoration would either have been imported from English monasteries or was imitated by Scottish monks who had seen English manuscripts. One manuscript perhaps written and decorated in Scotland is a copy of Boethius' *Consolation of Philsosophy* in Glasgow University Library. The charter of Malcolm IV of 1159 confirming grants to Kelso Abbey is Scottish and was probably made at Kelso. Two manuscripts with Scottish medieval provenances made at the end of the 12th century show how Scottish manuscript art followed the development of Gothic manuscript art in England. The Iona Psalter, commissioned at Oxford for a nun at Iona Nunnery, has delicate, painted, zoomorphic and scrollwork decoration which is echoed in the Blantyre Psalter made in Scotland for someone connected with a Scottish Augustinian house. It is possible that the Iona book

or a manuscript like it from England served as a model. Only one other surviving manuscript, the Lesmahagow Missal, is likely to have been made in Scotland in this period, the few other manuscripts of the 13th century with Scottish medieval provenances being imported from England, Northern France or Flanders.

While the illumination of manuscripts was carried out exclusively in the monasteries, the new burghs were centres of craftsmanship in metal, wood and leather. Some of the names of the early craftsmen are known to us, for example Baldwin the Lorimer, a Fleming who made trappings for David I's horses. It is not impossible that the fine prick spur found in recent excavations in Perth came from his workshop. Some pieces of metalwork of the period show an identifiably Scottish style. One such artifact, the bell shrine from Kilmichael Glassary in Argyll, is ornamented with an interesting fusion of Romanesque, Irish and Norse decorative traditions.

The first Scottish coinage was struck under David I, to begin with at Carlisle by English moneyers and later at Roxburgh, Berwick and elsewhere. The earliest coins can best be described as barbarous, on the whole of crude design and rough execution, unlike the very fine seals (mostly in the form of impressions) which survive. Most of these are very competent pieces of work and are of considerable

13

artistic merit like the twelfth-century seal of Edward of Restalrig which shows a lively scene of David rescuing the lamb from the lion's jaws.

During this period, however, many luxury items were imported. The beautiful enamelled and gilt Balfour Ciborium, which probably belonged to a church in the North East, was probably made in England and the Whithorn Crozier is also likely to have been made either in England or France rather than Scotland. The chessmen found in Lewis in the Outer Hebrides may be imports, although their Scandinavian style does not altogether preclude the possibility that they were made in these Isles.

B2   Capital with masks

B1   Capital

Scotland 12th Century
0.31×0.51×0.48 m
From St Brides Church, Douglas, Lanarkshire.
Scottish Development Department

A capital carved in a Corinthian style with tiers of acanthus-like leaves and volutes bordered by bands of beading. In the centre of each face is a rosette. The abacus is badly damaged.

Richardson, *The Mediaeval Stone Carver in Scotland*, 17–18

B2   Capital with masks

Scotland 12th century
0.55×0.79×0.47 m
From St Brides Church, Douglas, Lanarkshire.
Scottish Development Department

A capital which was possibly that of the main respond of the chancel arch in an earlier church on the site. It has grotesque heads or masks at the corners separated by a palmette motif on each face. The masks have prominent ears and eyes. From their mouths issue the stems of the palmettes.

Richardson, *The Mediaeval Stone Carver in Scotland*, 18

Jedburgh Abbey, architectural and sculptural fragments

Scotland 12th century
Scottish Development Department

The Augustinian house of Jedburgh, Roxburghshire, was founded by David I, probably shortly before 1139, the date of a charter of confirmation granted by that king. There was already a church on the site which probably served until the abbey church was complete enough for use. Its transepts and the inner parts of the choir were built in the Norman style, but the design from the crossing westwards is transitional. The main building campaign was to continue into the middle of the 13th century. The situation of Jedburgh Abbey close to the English Border meant that it was subject to many raids throughout the next four centuries. The church was almost constantly being repaired. In 1552 the monastery was finally suppressed, but part of the nave of the great abbey church continued to be used as the Parish Kirk until 1870.

Roxburgh Inv, no 414

B3   *Figure Fragment*

Mid 12th century
0.34×0.29×0.20 m

The western portal of Jedburgh Abbey is related to that of Rochester (*c.* 1150). At Rochester there are single figures on each ingo or recessed face of the doorway, and it has been suggested that this draped figure occupied a corresponding position on the jambs of the west portal at Jedburgh. All that remains of this figure is the torso, clad in 'damp-fold' drapery.

B4   *Cushion Capital*

Early 12th century
0.31×0.23×0.21 m

A trumpet-shaped 'cubic' or 'cushion' capital ornamented with large beading and surmounted by a simple moulded abacus. It comes from an angle shaft and may belong to an earlier phase of building than is now represented at the abbey.

B3 Figure Fragment

B4 Cushion Capital

B5 *Scallop Capital*

Mid 12th century
0.32×0.26×0.195 m
A scallop capital similar to those used in the east end
of the abbey church. This one, however, is carved
with a crenellated design and may come from the
conventual buildings. Scallop capitals are derived
from the cushion form.

B6 *Waterleaf Capital*

Last quarter of 12th century
0.35×0.25×0.22 m

A capital from an angle-shaft of the 'waterleaf'
variety, with tiny volutes at its angles. They were
used in the nave and triforium arcades of the abbey
church and are characteristic of transitional work.
Similar capitals were used at Selby Abbey in
Yorkshire.

B6 Waterleaf Capital

B7–9 *Two Door-Rybats and a Voussoir*

Late 12th century
0.48×0.39×0.16 m
0.69×0.35×0.31 m
0.36×0.22×0.17 m

One of the rybats has a clasping chevron design,
the other a foliate pattern. The voussoir is decorated
with a palmette enclosed in a chevron and has a roll
moulding at the angle. All three probably formed
part of the parish door–none of which remains *in
situ*–in the north aisle wall of the nave.

Dunfermline Abbey, architectural fragments

Scotland 12th century
Scottish Development Department

The present abbey church at Dunfermline, Fife, of
which only the nave survives, is largely the work of
David I, and was dedicated in 1150. Dunfermline
was a favourite royal centre and many of the royal
family were buried there, including Malcolm III, St
Margaret and Robert Bruce.

Fife Inv., no 197

B10 *Volute Capital*

1st half 12th century
0.29×0.285×0.14 m

This capital has volutes at the corners, curled
downwards. It is derived ultimately from the
classical Corinthian type.

B11 *Scallop Capital*

1st half 12th century
0.40×0.40×0.31 m

A capital for a wall shaft, with scallops and vertical
strips of beading.

B7　Two Door-Rybats and a Voussoir

B10　Volute Capital

B12　*Double Nook-Shaft*

1st half 12th century
1.10×0.28×0.15 m

Both shafts are decorated with chevrons and probably flanked a window.

B13　**Voussoir**

Scotland 12th century
0.33×0.15×0.42 m

From Kirknewton Church, Midlothian, demolished in 1780.
Edinburgh, National Museum

The voussoir represents a section of two orders of the archivolts which surmounted the portal of the Norman church of Kirknewton. The inner archivolt would have been decorated with the chevron motif, the outer with a series of individual motifs or figures; in this are a bearded man and a woman. The style is rather crude and linear.

B14　**Stoup**

Scotland 12th century
0.36 m diam. 0.84 m h
From Herdmanstoun House Chapel, East Lothian. Probably originally made for a church nearby.
Edinburgh, National Museum L. 1956–12

The stoup, which contained holy water and stood near the door of the church, was engaged with the wall from which it projected and has therefore been carved on three sides only.

The basin and support are carved from one block, and resemble an elaborate Romanesque column with four engaged shafts surmounted by a multicubical capital.

East Lothian Inv, 106–7

B15　**Stone basin**

Scotland Early 13th century
0.53×0.53×0.38 m
Dryburgh Abbey, Berwickshire
Scottish Development Department

A rectangular stone basin usually assumed to be a font. It may have been lined with metal as the small sockets for dowels suggest. Alternatively it may have formed the socket of a free standing monument or cross or may have been part of a container for a heart burial. Each of the vertical sides is carved with a design of high quality representing two wyverns. They have bird-like bodies with long snake-like necks interlacing at the angles and terminating in

　　　　B11　Scallop Capital

B15   Stone basin

B16   St Margaret's gospels

heads which grasp ascending branches. Their long tails divide into slender branches, developing in turn into palmetted flowers and buds.

Richardson, *The Mediaeval Stone Carver in Scotland*, 33–34

B16   St Margaret's gospels

England *c.* 1025–1050
190×240 mm
Oxford, Bodleian Library Lat lit F5

The book, decorated with full-page portraits of the Evangelists, in a style typical of late Anglo-Saxon illustration modelled on Carolingian book paintings, is probably the Gospel book of Queen Margaret, mentioned by her chaplain Turgot in his account of her life.

Madan & Craster, *Western MSS*, no 29744

B17   Glossed Matthew

France? 12th century
248×150 mm
ex Isle of May Priory
Oxford, St John's College No 111

The manuscript has marginal (unfinished) drawings of Christ on the cross which date to the second half of the twelfth century.

James, *MSS in St John's College*, 144

B18   Writings of St Augustine

England 12th century
245×150 mm
ex Kelso Abbey
Dublin, Trinity College no 226

The manuscript has several initials decorated with Romanesque animal and vegetal designs, some of which are painted. It is probably not Scottish work but was at Kelso Abbey in the twelfth century.

Abbot, *MSS in Trinity College*, 32

B19   Charter of Malcolm IV to Kelso Abbey

Scotland 1159
775×580 mm
ex Kelso Abbey
The Duke of Roxburghe (per the National Library of Scotland)

The charter confirms grants of Malcolm IV to Kelso Abbey. It is decorated with a large initial M for Malcolm formed of snake-like beasts framing two enthroned figures, David, the founder of the Abbey, and Malcolm, his grandson, painted with bold colours and gold. The style, which consists of strong outlines for the drapery and other features of the figures, combined with a system of highlights and flat areas of colour for the background, conforms to contemporary English Romanesque manuscript art.

The artist is likely to have been either a monk at

the abbey or an official of the royal chancery.

Boase, *English Art*, 154; Rickert, *Painting in Britain*, 228.

B20 Dialogues of St Gregory

England 12th century
250×390 mm
Edinburgh, University Library no 101

The manuscript is decorated with coloured capitals and book initials. There are two additions bound with it; a leaf from a fourteenth-century antiphoner of York use and two leaves from a French manuscript of the fifteenth century. It was at Sweetheart Abbey by the fifteenth century.

Borland, *Western Medieval MSS*, 159–60

B21 Boethius, De Consolatione Philosophiae

England or Scotland, *c*. 1125–1150
255×385 mm
Glasgow, University Library Hunter 279

A copy of Boethius' *Consolation of Philosophy* probably made in Scotland for a monastery library.

It is decorated on several pages with vigorous Romanesque drawings, one of which is an initial made up of fighting, interlaced animals. The manuscript was in Scotland by the twelfth century.

Young & Aitken, *MSS in the Hunterian Museum*, 225

B22 The Iona psalter

England *c*. 1200
300×420 mm
Edinburgh National Library of Scotland no 10000

The Psalter has initials illuminated with coloured paint and gold. Perhaps its finest feature is the large framed initial B which opens Psalm 1. This is infilled with fine scrolls of foliage in which several small white beasts like lions are entangled. The background is patterned and gold is applied. The roundels at the corners of the frame show David playing the harp, and three musicians.

The Psalter was made in England for someone in a Scottish Augustinian House, possibly for a nun at Iona Abbey. The calendar and litany contain many Iona Saints.

McRoberts, *Scottish Medieval Liturgical Books*, no 9

B19 Charter of Malcolm IV to Kelso Abbey

B22   The Iona psalter

B23   The Blantyre psalter

Scotland? 12th–13th century
320×420 mm
Durham University Library Bamburgh Castle Coll.
Select 6

The psalter, made for someone connected with a Scottish Augustinian house, has elaborate initial illumination consisting of vegetal scrolls and zoomorphic elements painted with gold, imitating initials in manuscripts made in England and France in the later twelfth century. In particular, the initial decoration of the psalter is close to some in the Iona Psalter which was made in England for someone in a Scottish Augustinian house.

It is probably Scottish work and may have been used at Blantyre, a monastic house attached to Holyrood Abbey.

Innes Rev, viii (1957), 75–85

B24   Kersmains Bell

B24   **Kersmains Bell**

Scotland 12th century
420×500 mm
Found during the ploughing of a field at Kersmains Farm near Kelso in 1973.
Edinburgh, National Museum KA

An early cast bronze tower-bell with a soundbow section of primitive form. The canons and argent of the bell have been broken from the crown. The corrosion of the metal has been caused by centuries of burial under soil. The bell had probably not been in use for very long; the clapper does not seem to have made much impression on the inside.

It is the only tower-bell of the twelfth century so far found in Scotland.

PSAS, cvii (1975–6), 275–8

B25   **The Balfour ciborium** (also known as the Kennet ciborium)

England 1165–1175
188×159 mm
Formerly in the collection of Lord Balfour of Burleigh.
London, Victoria and Albert Museum

The ciborium is composed of two parts, a bowl and a cover with a knop, made of copper and richly decorated with champlevé enamel and gilding. The decorative scheme combines foliaceous ornament composed of scrolls and leaves, with a series of medallions, six each on the bowl and lid. Those on the bowl enclose subjects from Old Testament history which prefigure the events in Our Lord's

B25 The Balfour Ciborium

history depicted on the lid. Thus the scenes may be 'read' in the following way:

The circumcision of Isaac–The Baptism of Our Lord

Preparation for the Sacrifice of Isaac–Our Lord bearing the cross

The Substitution of a ram for Isaac, for the Sacrifice–The Crucifixion

Samson escaping from the gates of Gaza–The Resurrection

David rescuing a lamb from a bear–'The Harrowing of Hell'

Elijah taken up into Heaven–The Ascension

The inscription engraved into the scrolls above and below the medallions comment on the events depicted.

The ciborium closely resembles two other approximately contemporary ciboria, the Malmesbury ciborium in the Pierpont Morgan Library in New York and the Warwick Ciborium in the Victoria and Albert Museum, which also have representations of the types and anti-types of the Life of Christ.

The Balfour ciborium is thought to be the only surviving altar vessel from the pre-Reformation church in Scotland. A tradition of the Clackmannan family of Balfour of Burleigh, to whom it has belonged since the sixteenth century, states that it was presented to Sir James Balfour by Mary Queen of Scots. The vessel may be identified as the 'coup and cover upper enamellit' which is listed in one of the inventories of Mary, Queen of Scots, and

interestingly this entry is to be found in a section of lists of the possessions of the Queen got as booty from Gordon Castle after the defeat of the Earl of Huntly at Corrichie in 1562. The booty included a great deal of ecclesiastical furnishings from Aberdeen Cathedral and other churches in the North East, which were stored in the Castle for safety.

Constable, *The Kennet Ciborium*

B26 The Whithorn crozier

England or France 1175–1200
200×90 mm
Found in one of two graves excavated at the 12th-century Premonstratensian church, Whithorn in Galloway.
Edinburgh, National Museum

The crozier head is formed of a tube of copper and has a metal flower-like cluster fixed at the centre of the crook with a peg. The stem is decorated with representations of figures, animals and vegetable motifs, each rendered in champlevé enamelling within a reticulated framework of raised gilded metal. The human figures on the crozier comprise representations of prophets, each of which holds a book or a scroll, and in the lowest part, four bishops dressed in episcopal garb. One of these, with a gilded nimbus, may be St Ninian (d 432 AD), the original founder of the church at Whithorn known as Candida Casa, which was replaced in the twelfth century by the Premonstratensian church where the crozier was found. The crozier probably belonged to a bishop of the See of Whithorn, active during the revival of the church there in the twelfth century. This may have been Christian, 1154–86, John 1189–1209, or Walter, who died in 1235.

An enamelled crozier head, of a similar size and decoration to the Whithorn crozier, dated 1175, was found in the Abbey of St Père en Vallé in Chartres. (Now in the Bargello, Florence).

Burlington Mag, (May 1967)

B27 Reliquary

Scotland Late 12th century
50×30 mm
Thought to have come from the church of Whithorn near Wigtown, Galloway. In a private collection for a number of years.
London, British Museum

A circular reliquary composed of two discs. One has a metal setting in the shape of a cross with fragments of the true cross within it, surrounded by river pearls sewn to the disc with gold wire. The other disc, which is damaged, is covered with a number of small

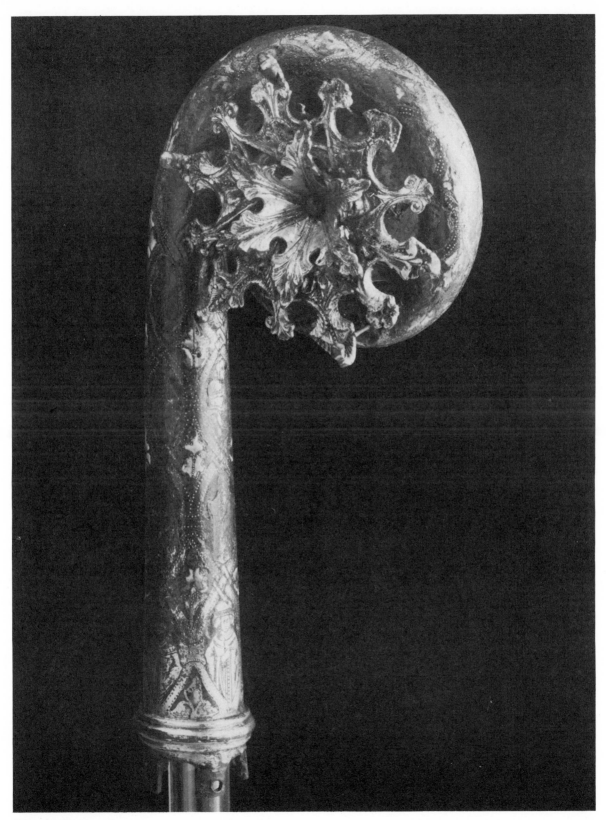

B26   The Whithorn Crozier

B27 Reliquary

settings some of which still hold relics. At the centre is another cross-shaped setting which probably also held a fragment of the True Cross. Both sides of the reliquary were once covered with lids, but only the first side still retains its cover, which is made of a domed block of crystal set in a gold mount. The crystal acts as a magnifying glass—increasing the apparent size of the pearls and relic behind it. The band of the enclosing ring bears an abbreviated inscription:

XSE XPSTI NINIANI ANDREW EX MAURIS GEORGII MERG' D'NOR FERG BO SE MARIE

It is a relic list starting with the 'True Cross' and finishing with the 'Blessed Virgin' in between which are St Ninian, Andrew of the Moors, St George, St Margaret, St Norbert, St Fergustian and St Boniface. The composition of the list which includes S.S. Ninian and Norbert, Archbishop of Magdeburg and founder of the Order of Premonstratensian Canons respectively, indicates that the reliquary emanated from a Premonstratensian church closely associated with St Ninian. This is likely to have been Whithorn or else Fearn in County Ross which was founded in the 1220s and colonized from Whithorn.

The reliquary was probably once suspended from a chain which was fitted to two loops, the remains of which are visible on the top of the rim.

Trans Dumfries & Galloway Archaeol Soc, xxxii (1953–4), 119–23

B28 Pyx and cover

Scotland 12th century
bowl 38×101 mm; cover 103 mm diam.
Found in digging a grave between the tower of St Regulus and the south corner of the east gable of the Cathedral, St Andrews.
Edinburgh, National Museum.

The pyx consists of a bowl and cover, both made of

beaten bronze. The bowl has a slightly flattened bottom which is engraved with a geometrical cross with double outlines within a circle. There is a similar pattern on the corresponding concave part of the exterior. The rim of the bowl which is slightly crushed on one side has a turned edge which is flattened to accommodate the lid. The latter has its edge turned down and is engraved with a border of four concentric circles enclosing a celtic cross.

A similar bowl without a lid was discovered with the Ardagh chalice, Ireland.

PSAS, xxxiii (1898–9), 76–78

B29 Censer

Scotland 11th or 12th century
87×100 mm, lily 50 mm
Said to have been found during excavations in the foundations of a house in Ferguston Muir, Bearsden near Glasgow in 1879.
Glasgow Art Gallery and Museum

The censer has an architectural design commonly produced at the end of the twelfth century. It is formed of two cast bronze parts fitted with projecting loops for suspension chains of which there were originally four. It is decorated with incised ornament on the bowl and cover and the latter is perforated with many round holes over its surface, including some which are made to resemble windows in the tower and gables of the church building at the top. The chains are attached to a conical-shaped lily which has concave sides decorated with four panels of anthropomorphic design.

The censer closely resembles another in the British Museum, and it is almost identical to a censer found at the chapel of Sven Grathe, near Viborg, Jutland, Denmark, now in the National Museum of Denmark.

Glasgow Archaeol Journ, i (1969), 43–46

B30 Three gold fillets

Scotland, 12th century
0.432 m, 0.343 m, 0.241 m.
Part of a hoard found on the Island of Bute in 1863 which also included 2 rings and a number of coins of David I of Scotland and Henry I and Stephen of England.
Edinburgh, National Museum FE 41–43

Three gold fillets ornamented with small punch marks along the edges and a zig zag and pellet decoration at the ends. The third, which is broken, has two zig zag lines forming a row of diamond shaped figures.

PSAS, v (1862–4), 215, 373

B29 Censer

B31 The Kilmichael Glassary bell-shrine

Scotland 12th century
95×85×148 mm
Found during the construction of a dyke at
Torrebhlaurn in the parish of Kilmichael Glassary in
Argyll *c.* 1814.
Edinburgh, National Museum KA 4

The bronze bell-shrine, which originally stood on
four animal headed feet, is composed of decorated
plates held together by continuous corner brackets
and a top plate which includes the handle and the
Manus Dei. There are loop handles on the sides and
on the front is fixed a cast bronze figure of Christ with
a crown, dressed in a loin cloth gathered up in a knot.

The shrine enclosed a small quadrangular iron bell
which could be touched by its devotees through a
circular hole in the bottom of the shrine case.

With it was found a small bronze cross and a
length of chain. The chain may once have been
divided into three lengths to connect three arms of
the cross with loops on the sides and in the *Manus Dei*
so that it could be hung or dangled from the hand.

The construction and decoration of the shrine,
including the fashioning of the animal head
terminals on the main handle, the animal headed
feet, the interlace pattern on one of the side plates
and the foliate triangles and lozenges on the corner
brackets, reflects a Scoto-Irish tradition of art. The
figure of Christ however resembles examples from
Scandinavia and N. Germany. The use of bronze in
the shrine to the exclusion of gems, silver additions,
and enamels is also characteristically Scandinavian.

PSAS, xliv (1909–10), 274–5

B32 Bronze Christ from crucifix

Scotland 12th century
100×38 mm
From McEwen's Castle, Cowal
Glasgow Art Galleries and Museums

Christ is crowned and has long hair and a beard. He
is naked but for a loin cloth. His arms have been bent
round behind his head, perhaps indicating that when
lost this piece was intended for the melting-pot.
Although not so finely modelled it is similar in style
to the Christ on the Kilmichael Glassary bell-shrine.

B31   The Kilmichael glassary bell-shrine

B32   Bronze Christ from crucifix

McEwen's Castle is a fortified promontory site and the crucifix was found in the remains of a turf house within it.

B33   Gilt bronze Christ from crucifix

Scotland? 12th century
125 mm
Found in a grave at Tibbermuir Churchyard, Perthshire.
Edinburgh, National Museum

Christ is represented in a loin cloth knotted at his right hip. He has long hair and a beard and wears a crown. The pose, and the serene expression on the face, are similar to the Christ of the Kilmichael Glassary bell-shrine though in detail the two are not similar.

B34   Bronze Christ from crucifix

Scotland 12th century
138 mm
From Dunvegan, Skye.
London, British Museum

This figure is crowned and wears a loin cloth. The feet are positioned one on top of the other with one nail driven through both.

B35   Bronze Christ from crucifix

Scotland 12th century
From Iona.
His Grace, the Duke of Argyll, Inverary Castle.

B36   Bronze Christ from crucifix

German? 13th century
140×130 mm
Said to have been found on Islay.
Edinburgh, National Museum KE 12

The figure, which is of cast bronze, originally formed part of an altar or processional crucifix to which it was fixed by nails through the hands and by a bronze tang at the back of the feet. The figure, which has long hair and a beard, is dressed in a loin cloth decorated with zig-zag lines and a long tied 'belt'. The garment may once have been decorated with enamel.

B37   Enamelled Christ from crucifix

France, Limoges 13th century
170×133 mm
Found in the churchyard of Ceres, Fife.
Edinburgh, National Museum KE 7

The figure, of bronze, decorated with gilding,

B34   Bronze Christ from crucifix

B36   Bronze Christ from crucifix

engraving and champlevé enamel, wears a crown and a two tiered gown which consists of a knee-length dalmatic tunic worn over a long undergarment which descends to the ankles. This representation of the crucified Christ resembles figures from crucifixes made in Limoges in the thirteenth century and belongs to a particular iconographical type–the 'Christ-King'.

PSAS, xvii (1882–3), 146–51

B38   Bronze figure of a saint

Scotland 12th century
104 mm
Found at the 'Druidical Circle', Holywood, Dumfries, near the site of Holywood Abbey.
Edinburgh, National Museum, KE 9 (Electrotype)

A bronze figure of a saint, holding a book and with his hand raised in blessing. It was probably attached to a book or reliquary.

PSAS, xvi (1881–2), 417–18.

B39   Fragment of a bronze dish

N. Germany, 12th century
now 254 mm diam.
Found in a ploughed field close to the moat around the Castle mound at Leuchars, Fife.
Edinburgh, National Museum NT 142

The fragment represents the central part of the bowl. It has an incised decoration consisting of a man in armour attacking a monster. Behind this main figure are the letters IRA and elsewhere, NA and VI. Five similar figures are placed radially around the one in the centre.

The fragment may be compared with engraved bronze bowls of the twelfth and thirteenth centuries which have been found in Britain and Europe, many of which seem to have been made in the region of the lower Rhine and the Meuse. In particular the designs on this fragment resemble those of the bronze bowl found in Sarah Street, Leicester in 1943 (Leicester Museum and Art Gallery), which is particularly like a bowl found in Elizabethstrasse, Aachen.

PSAS, lxvi (1931–32), 15 and fig 2

B40 Tableman

Scotland 11th–12th century
38 mm
Found under the stone flooring of the hall at Dalcross Castle, Inverness-shire.
Edinburgh, National Museum

The playing piece is made of bone and is carved with a grotesque figure holding its tail over its shoulder.

It bears a strong resemblance to a tableman from Stonehaven which is carved with a figure like a centaur holding its tail, and also a playing piece in the Victoria and Albert Museum (A 100–1927).

PSAS, xxxi (1896–7), 80

B41 Bone tableman

Scotland 11th or 12th centuries
40 mm
London, Victoria and Albert Museum A 100–1927

A playing-piece carved on the front with a beast like a griffon, holding a long tail over its shoulder which appears to terminate in another head. The design is similar to the playing-piece found at Dalcross Castle

(Edinburgh, National Museum). The form of the beast seems to be Scandinavian.

Beckwith, *Ivory Carvings*, no 110

B41 Bone tableman

B42 The Lewis chessmen

Scandinavian, possible Anglo-Scandinavian Late 12th century
Heights vary from about 60 mm to over 100 mm
Found in 1831 on the west coast of Lewis in the Outer Hebrides in a sandbank at Uig.

The *British Museum*, London, has 67 chessmen (plus a belt buckle and 14 plain draughtsmen) and the *National Museum*, Edinburgh, has 11.

All the pieces are made of walrus ivory and there are enough for four sets, except a knight, 4 rooks and 45 pawns. Some of the pieces seem to have been stained to indicate the 'black' side. Only the pawns are abstract, the kings, queens, knights, etc, being carved as people in the dress of the period.

All are probably the products of the one workshop and the Scandinavian character of the carving has long been recognised, particularly the warriors (=castles or rooks) biting the top edge of their shields in the 'berserker' manner. The foliage carving, especially on the thrones of the kings, queens and bishops, is similar to that on a small group of walrus ivory carvings of Scandinavian manufacture.

Until 1266 the Western Isles of Scotland were ruled from Norway.

Taylor, *The Lewis Chessmen*

B43 Walrus ivory chessmen

North Europe Mid 13th century
92×62 mm
Found in Skye?
Edinburgh, National Museum NS 15

B43 Walrus ivory chessmen

The piece consists of two mail-clad figures seated back to back, supported by a framework of interlaced branches terminating in foliage. Each carries a sword in his right hand and a shield over his left. Although the carving of the two warriors is vigorous, the foliage is flat and more conservative in style–typically Romanesque. Amongst it is a small pine-cone surrounded by leaves which might represent the trademark of a particular workshop. A similar element links the Lewis chessmen with other walrus ivory carvings having a Scandinavian provenance.

Goldschmidt, *Die Elfenbeinskulpturen*, no 257

B44 Seal matrix of mounted knight in mail armour

Scotland 12th century
Diam. 62 mm
From Raewick, Shetland.
Edinburgh, National Museum NM42

This brass matrix has a conventional, but spirited, representation of a mounted knight.
Legend: SIGIL BENEDICAMVS DCI ANNV FIL
Not all the letters are the right way round and the brass disc of the matrix seems to have been cut from something else. It may be a trial piece.

28

B44 Seal matrix of mounted knight in mail armour

3 A GOLDEN AGE

The period from the middle to the latter part of the thirteenth century was one of great prosperity for Scotland. The reigns of David I's successors were relatively peaceful. The growing mercantile communities in the burghs were bringing wealth into the country as a result of expanding overseas trade. In this period also, patronage of the arts reached new heights, with a wider spectrum of society enjoying a greater variety and quality of material culture produced either locally or imported from abroad.

The enthusiasm for church building in Scotland which had characterized the previous century continued. Monastic and secular churches were constructed on a grand scale. The Abbeys of Dundrennan, Arbroath and Inchcolme as well as Coldingham Priory were brought largely to completion before the middle of the century. Sweetheart Abbey was commenced in the 1280s. The great Cathedrals of Glasgow, Elgin and Dunblane also belong to this era. As in the twelfth century the influence of architecture from south of the border was predominant although Scottish architects never entirely embraced the spirit of Gothic architecture as it was exemplified at the time in England. Nevertheless the achievements of the period are marked by imagination and daring. Although timber-roofing still prevailed over stone-vaulting there were sections of skilful ribbed and groin vaulting at Jedburgh and Holyrood Abbeys, at Elgin Cathedral and in Glasgow Cathedral crypt.

Glasgow Cathedral, despite being roofed in the nave and choir, is in all respects a great Gothic cathedral. It has a magnificent well proportioned choir with an elegant window of four lancets in the east gable. From the capitals of the piers in the choir wall shafts rise to the top of the wall dividing the arcade, triforium and clerestory into high vertical bays. Dunblane Cathedral is a small building with no transepts and no clerestory, but the low nave is carefully designed and has a distinctively Gothic sense of unity. The west front of the cathedral has one of the finest features of Scottish architecture of the time: a deeply recessed central door flanked by two sharply pointed blind arches on each side.

The great west doorway at Elgin Cathedral follows quite a different design. Here there is a recessed double door, contained within an obtusely pointed arch of several narrow orders rising from a succession of nine shafts and mouldings. It is crowned by three gablets with niches. The choir of the cathedral, which dates to the late thirteenth century, has an east gable taken up almost entirely with windows, two tiers of single windows and a great rose window at the top vaulting.

With the outbreak of the Wars of Independence in 1296 the building of churches in Scotland came to a halt and between then and the end of the fourteenth century practically nothing worthy of note was constructed. Meanwhile many buildings were destroyed or badly damaged by the English or Scots.

Dunblane Cathedral, nave, 13th century

The prolonged conflict with England also meant that English influence in the fields of art and architecture waned.

While contacts with England were almost entirely cut off, trade with France and Flanders flourished. Among the imports from these countries were some manuscripts which probably included the *Ramsey Psalter*. Metalwork was also coming to Scotland from the Continent: enamelled crucifixes and candle-sticks, for example, made in the famous metal-working centre of Limoges have been found in Scotland. Scotland of course already had skilled metal-workers of her own and was not dependent for all her quality products on foreign imports. The number of fine Scottish-made brooches, rings and spoons found dating to the thirteenth century testifies to this.

The looting and destruction of most of the major burghs during the wars with England must have disrupted the activities of tradesmen and craftsmen and on occasion there was dreadful slaughter, as when Edward I brutally took Berwick in 1296. Nevertheless the years of poverty and hardships of the mid-14th century had not yet arrived and the Scots even made considerable gains from the wars. The greatest of these accompanied the victory of Bannockburn in 1314, of which it was said that 'Scotland became rich in one day'. The booty collected after the rout of the English included jewels, vestments, rich furnishing and military stores and equipment, as well as ransom money for the release of captured English barons. The Bute or Bannatyne Mazer and Savernake Horn date from this period. The Mazer with its remarkable print decorated with shields and a lion couchant is likely to be linked with King Robert Bruce, and may have been made for the celebrations of the victory at Bannockburn or perhaps the marriage of Bruce's daughter Marjory to the High Steward in 1318. Despite its similarity to some Flemish mazers and vessels there is good reason to think it is of Scottish workmanship. If this is indeed the case it suggests that not all craftsmen of quality were put out of business as a result of the wars.

Elgin Cathedral, architectural and sculptural fragments

Scotland 13th–14th century
Scottish Development Department

In July 1224 the cathedral of the diocese of Moray was transferred from Spynie to the church of the Holy Trinity beside Elgin. Work was begun immediately on a new church which incorporated the transepts of the older one on the site. After a severe fire in 1270 the cathedral was reconstructed to its present dimensions, with double aisles in the nave, transepts and a crossing tower, an aisled choir and flat ended presbytery. The chapter house was built at this time as well. Despite the vicious sack of the church by Alexander Stewart, 'The Wolf of Badenoch', in 1390, it retained the plan and Gothic appearance given to it in the thirteenth century. Decay and neglect set in after the Reformation in the middle of the sixteenth century, but enough remains today to show why it justified being called the finest cathedral in Scotland by more than one 16th-century Scottish historian.

Richardson and MacIntosh, *Elgin Cathedral*

C1   *Corbel with figure*

Scotland Late 13th–Early 14th century
0.23×0.56×0.43 m

The front of the corbel is carved with a standing figure of a cleric holding an open book. Under his feet is the head of a lion. Possibly St Mark is intended.

C2 Boss with seated figure

C2 *Boss with seated figure*

Scotland Late 13th–Early 14th century
0.23×0.56×0.43 m

The boss, now badly damaged, is carved with a seated figure encircled by a spray of foliage. From the aisle vaulting.

C3–4 *Bosses with beasts*

Scotland Late 13th–Early 14th century
0.56×0.33 m
0.34×0.47×0.41 m

Two bosses from the aisle vaults carved with snake-like creatures in foliage.

C5–6 *Capitals with foliage*

Scotland Late 13th–Early 14th century
0.70×0.26 m
0.70×0.26 m

Two capitals carved with foliage, one with two rows of eight petalled flowers. Both probably supported the aisle arcades.

C7 **Capital**

Scotland 13th century
0.33×0.38×0.17 m
Provenance unknown
Edinburgh, National Museum

Capital for a wall-shaft, with stiff-leaf foliage.

C8 **Roof boss**

Scotland 13th century
0.36×0.30×0.26 m
Jedburgh Abbey, Roxburghshire
Scottish Development Department

A foliate roof boss which formed the intersection of two vaulting ribs. It comes from the chapterhouse.

C9–10 **Two roof bosses with heads**

Scotland Mid 13th century
0.38×0.38×0.17 m
0.38×0.38×0.15 m
Glasgow Cathedral, Laigh Church
Glasgow Art Galleries and Museums (casts)

On both bosses a head is framed by a wreath of leaves. They are traditionally thought to represent David Comyn and Isabella de Valognes, benefactors of the church.

C11 **Head of Christ**

Scotland Early 13th century
0.28 m
St Andrews Cathedral
Scottish Development Department

Head of Christ carved in sandstone, with long flowing hair.

C3 Bosses with beast

C12 Marble graveslab with indents for brass

The Low Countries, Tournai Early 14th century
2.90×1.42 m
From Dundrennan Abbey, Kirkcudbrightshire.
Edinburgh, National Museum (photographic assemblage)

This graveslab, depicting a knight and lady, was originally inset in brass, with the faces and hands of both figures inserted in alabaster, marble, or some other material requiring a specially deep indent. Only the outline of these and the brasses now remains in the stone—enough to indicate that the monument was of high quality.

C13 Effigy of Sir James Douglas

Scotland *c.* 1330
2.40×0.72 m
Douglas, St Brides Church

This effigy is of a knight dressed in a mail hauberk, chausses (leggings) and coif (helmet). Over the hauberk he wears a long flowing surcoat and he is armed with a sword and shield. There is a small lion crouching at his feet.

Most Scottish effigies are carved as solemn, passive figures, gazing on eternity with equanimity. By contrast there is an attempt to create a certain amount of dynamism about this one from Douglas, an effect enhanced by the way his hand grasps his sword hilt in its scabbard, as if on the point of

unsheathing it. This type of image is undoubtedly derived from English models but is particularly appropriate in the case of Sir James Douglas. The 'Good Sir James', patriot and companion of Robert Bruce, was one of the most noted soldiers of his time. He died fighting to the last in Spain in 1330, taking the heart of Bruce to the Holy Land.

PSAS, xxix (1894–5), 345–8

C14 Sandstone head

Scotland Early 14th century
80×100 mm
From Culross Abbey, Fife.
Edinburgh, National Museum KJ 93

The head of an ecclesiastic carved in sandstone. He has a fillet or corona encircling his head and an amice round his neck.

PSAS, lviii (1923–4), 19

C15 Fragments of King Robert Bruce's tomb

France Early 14th century
Dunfermline Abbey, Fife
Edinburgh, National Museum KG 65–8, 70–1, 74

The tomb, which was placed in front of the high altar in the Abbey Church of Dunfermline, had long disappeared before the grave of Robert I was identified in 1821. It was commissioned during the King's life time and was carved in Paris by the sculptor, Thomas of Chartres, who was provided with alabaster, probably brought from England where there was an alabaster carving industry based in Nottingham.

The tomb would undoubtedly have been splendid. Traces of gilding still remain on some fragments. According to the Exchequer Rolls of Scotland the gold leaf for this was bought in Newcastle and York.

Archaeologia Scotica, ii (1822), 435ff

C16 Gratian, Concorda discordantium canonum

Scotland? Early 13th century
405×600 mm
ex Beauly Priory
Faculty of Advocates (per the National Library of Scotland) Advocates 3.1.12

The manuscript is decorated with illuminated initials on coloured backgrounds with internal grounds of gold. Gratian was the 12th-century founder of the science of Canon Law.

Ker, *Medieval Libraries*, 9, 229.

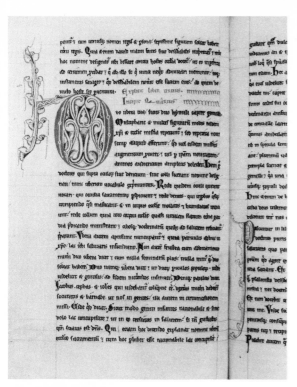

C17 Bede on song of songs

C17 **Bede on song of songs**

Scotland? Early 13th century
300×380 mm
ex Lindores Abbey
London, Gray's Inn no 5

This copy of Bede's commentary on the Song of Songs was probably written at the Cistercian abbey of Lindores, Fife. At the foot of folio 153v is the inscription 'Hic est liber sancte Marie et Sancti Andres de Lundores', in a hand matching that of the main text.

It is ornamented with initials embellished with pen work and some wash decoration.

Ker, *Medieval MSS*, i, 56

C18 **The Lesmahagow missal**

Scotland *c*. 1225–1250
240×380 mm
Edinburgh, National Library of Scotland Acc 2710

Only two pages of illuminated decoration survive in the missal at the opening of the Canon of the Mass. The decoration of the initials, which consists of thick foliage scrolls, is not sophisticated.

The missal was made for use in the Tironensian house of Lesmahagow, Lanarkshire.

McRoberts, *Scottish Medieval Liturgical Books*, no 10

C19 **Bible**

England? *c*. 1250–1300
320×420 mm
ex Cambuskenneth Abbey
Glasgow, University Library MS Gen 1126

The bible has decorated initials with plant scrolls and animal heads and also one surviving historiated initial. It was probably made in England.

C20 **Breviary**

England or Scotland? *c*. 1270
300×400 mm
ex Coldingham Priory?
London, British Library Harley 4664

The book has a number of historiated initials and also a large miniature showing the Virgin and Child adored by a Benedictine monk. The style of the painting is characteristic of English Gothic after 1250. The breviary was perhaps written at Durham.

Cat. Harleian MSS, iii, 1808–12

C21 **Psalter**

The Low Countries? Later 13th century
210×350 mm
ex Inchmahome Priory
Joanna Gordon (per the National Library of Scotland)
Dep 273

The Psalter is decorated with initials showing dragons and masks and other objects, with gold.

McRoberts, *Scottish Medieval Liturgical Books*, no 29

C22 **Bible**

North France or England? 2nd half 13th century
3 vols. 320×460 mm
ex Sweetheart Abbey, Kirkcudbrightshire
Princeton, University Library, USA

This is a high quality piece of work, decorated throughout with historiated initials in gold and colours and figures in the margins. It was at Sweetheart Abbey at an early date. Two volumes are decorated by different artists.

C23 **Liturgical calendar** (*July to October only*)

Scotland 1200–1250
440–350 mm
ex Holyrood Abbey
Edinburgh, National Library of Scotland no 5048

Two leaves from a calendar which originally formed part of a psalter or missal. The calendar was designed for Augustinian use and it seems to have been made

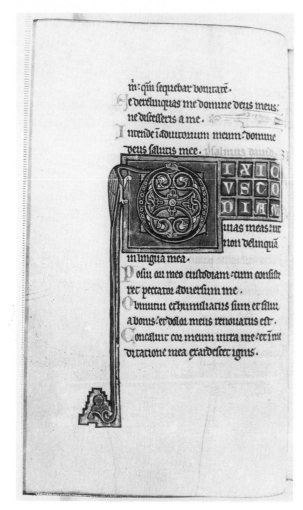

C21 Psalter

The psalter has decorated initials and marginal decoration including bas-de-page illustrations of hunting dogs chasing hares. It was probably made in Flanders but by the fifteenth century it was in Scotland where it was used by the Ramsay's of Colluthie in the Parish of Moonzie, near Cupar, Fife.

McRoberts, *Scottish Medieval Liturgical Books*, no 17

C25 Avicenna

England? 13th century
400×560 mm
ex Soulseat Abbey, Wigtownshire
Edinburgh University Library no 165

The manuscript is decorated throughout with boldly executed historiated initials in gold and colours. It is probably English and was in use in Scotland by the sixteenth century. Avicenna was an 11th-century Arab philosopher whose work was widely read in the Middle Ages.

Borland, *Western Medieval MSS*, 248–9

C26 The Murthly hours

England and France? Late 13th century
210×320 mm
Rothesay, Mount Stuart, Collection of the Marquess of Bute

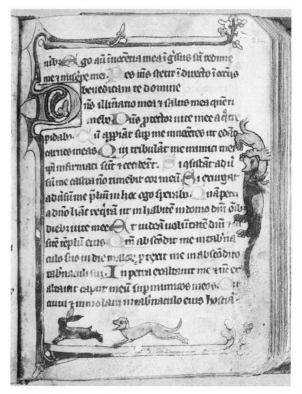

C24 The Ramsay psalter

for Holyrood Abbey. It contains S.S. Serf and Ninian and the feast of the relics of the Holy Cross.

At a later time the calendar must have moved away from Holyrood and Augustinian hands for certain relevant feasts and saints have been deleted. There are also a number of additions which point to its use in England.

At the top of each month is a large KL monogram decorated in colours and gold. The entries are written in red, green or blue.

PSAS, lxix (1934–5), 471–9; McRoberts, *Scottish Medieval Liturgical Books*, no 11

C24 The Ramsay psalter

The Low Countries Late 13th–14th centuries
Edinburgh, National Library of Scotland Advocates 18.8.8

C26 The Murthly hours

A Book of Hours lavishly decorated with miniatures in gold and colours with scenes from the Life of Christ and pages with large historiated initials and border illustrations. It is thought that the miniatures, which may have been taken from another manuscript, could be by an English hand. One of these, which shows the Roman soldiers guarding the sepulchre, has the coats of arms of various Scottish families, including Streathearn and Blair, emblazoned on the soldiers' shields. The rest of the manuscript was probably made in France.

The book of hours was in Scotland by the fifteenth century and was for a long time in the possession of the Murthly family.

McRoberts, *Scottish Medieval Liturgical Books*, no 23

C27 The Taymouth hours

England *c.* 1323–40
180×250 mm
London, British Library Yates Thomson 13

This Book of Hours was made in England and is richly decorated with bas-de-page illustrations of religious, and secular objects as well as scenes from romances, miniatures, and also a calendar ornamented with medallions of the zodiac and the labours of the months.

Books of Hours became very popular as devotional books from the thirteenth century. They were commissioned by wealthy patrons and designed to entertain their owners, tending usually to be lavishly decorated.

The Taymouth hours was probably made for Joan, daughter of Edward II, King of England, and wife of David I of Scotland. It was in Scotland certainly by the sixteenth century.

McRoberts, *Scottish Medieval Liturgical Books*, no 31

C27 The Taymouth hours

C28 Breviary

England? Early 14th century
220×310 mm
Edinburgh University Library no 27

The breviary has historiated initials painted in gold and colours, and borders decorated with animals and grotesques.

The manuscript came into Scottish hands at an early date, perhaps during the Wars of Independence. There are additions of two chronicles of Scottish history and insertions of saints and obits in the calendar. Many of these are connected with Aberdeen and the North, for example, St Machar.

Borland, *Western Medieval MSS*, 38–41

C29 New Testament in English

England Early 14th century
290×370 mm
Oxford, Bodleian Library Fairfax 11
The book once belonged to the Sinclair's of Roslin. It is decorated with well-painted initials and borders.

Madan & Craster, *Western MSS*, no 3891

C30 The Savernake horn and baldric

Horn—England or Scotland 13th century
Baldric—Scotland 14th century
horn 0.60 m
The earliest record of the horn is in a genealogy of the Earls of Hertford in William Camden's *Britannia* of 1607, where it is stated that it was transferred to the Seymour Earls of Hertford with the wardenship of the Forest of Savernake. An illustration of the horn together with the Scottish baldric appears also in the genealogy although the baldric is not mentioned in the text. The earlier provenance of the horn has not been ascertained. It is possible that the horn and baldric were in fact taken as booty by the Earl of Hertford from Edinburgh during the English offensive against Scotland in 1544.
London, British Museum

The horn is carved from an elephant's tusk and has a faceted surface decorated with ornamental fittings. At the mouth of the horn are two remarkable mounts, enamelled in the *basse taillé* method showing a series of hunting animals and hounds represented in individual sections. The quality of these enamels, which may be French, is very high. The other mounts on the horn are of recent date.

The larger of the two original mounts has a narrow flange on its outer extremity with representations of birds. There are also three figures, a king, a bishop and a forester blowing a horn, on the main part of the

mount, which may suggest that the horn played some part in an agreement between a king and a bishop concerning hunting land. On the opposite side of the mount is a lion sejant, the symbol of royalty.

The baldric attached to the horn probably replaced an earlier strap. It is made of leather and consists of a shoulder strap buckled to an H-shaped harness, with hook plates, one of which is engraved with a stag couchant, and a hinged mount enamelled

C30 The Savernake horn and baldric

with a lion couchant, a moth and two herons. There are thirteen silver fittings bearing a single coat of arms; argent, three cushions lozenge-ways gules with a tressure flory-counter flory gules, which are the arms of the Randolph Earls of Moray (created 1312). Thomas Randolph, first Earl of Moray was brother-in-law of Robert Bruce and one of his leading companions at arms.

The Earls of Moray had hunting lands in Morayshire and the cartulary of Elgin Cathedral of the fourteenth century (*Moray Registrum*) bears witness to disputes between the Bishop of Elgin and the family concerning rights to forest lands around the cathedral. It is not unlikely that such arguments may have preceded or succeeded an agreement presided over by the king between the bishop and the Earls of Moray, confirmed by the presentation of a horn to which the baldric was attached.

Brit Mus Yearbook, ii (1977), 201–211, pls iii & iv

C31   The Bute, or Bannatyne, mazer

Scotland? 14th century with additions of 16th century
250 mm
Probably originally the property of the Fitzgilberts who owned lands on the Isle of Bute. It passed to the Bannatyne family in the early sixteenth century, then in succession to the Macleods and to the MacGregors. It is now the property of the Marquisses of Bute.
Edinburgh, National Museum (on loan)

The Mazer is made of 'eyed' maple wood and has a remarkable silver gilt boss surmounted by a lion couchant in high relief and set with six enamelled shields. The ground of the boss is engraved with a strawberry plant motif, wyverns and cinquefoils. The tinctures of the arms represented on the shields enable this part of the Mazer to be dated to the

C31   The Bute, or Bannatyne, Mazer

second decade of the fourteenth century. The arms represent the following families: 1) (between the forepaws of the Lion) the High Steward—fess chequy azure and argent. 2) Douglas—argent on a chief azure three stars of the field (these arms predate the addition of the heart). 3) Fitzgilbert of Hamilton—gules three cinquefoils ermine. 4) a cadet of the House of Fitzgilbert—gules, a chevron ermine between three cinquefoils or. 5) Crawford—gules, a fess ermine. 6) Menteith (a branch of the Stewart family)—or, a band chequy sable and argent.

The shields, which have been inserted into the boss on round discs, may have been made in another workshop. The foot of the bowl, the six ornamental hinged straps and the rim, all of silver, thought to have been added to the mazer in the sixteenth century, are likely to have been commissioned by Ninian Bannatyne Lord of Kames whose name is engraved on the rim and who succeeded his father Robert in 1522.

The Mazer functioned as a communal drinking cup passed around a table at a meal where, it would appear, the nobles whose households are represented on the boss were present. It has been suggested that the lion and the circle of shields represent Robert Bruce surrounded by his vassals and that the mazer was commissioned by the High Steward for an occasion at his castle in Rothesay when Bruce was present. The keeper of Rothesay Castle was a member of the Fitzgilbert family, John 'son of Gilbert'. This was probably a hereditary position. A suitable occasion may have followed the victory of the Battle of Bannockburn in which the High Steward had a high command, or perhaps the marriage of the High Steward to Marjorie, Robert I's daughter.

PSAS, lxv (1930–1), 217–55

C32   The Kames brooch

Scotland *c.* 1300
27 mm
Kept with the Bute Mazer by the MacGregors of MacGregor who inherited both from the MacLeods of Bernera.
Edinburgh, National Museum

A gold ring brooch cast with the upper side forming a chain of six wyverns each gripping the one in front with left fore-paw and teeth and curling its tail around the neck of the one behind. On the flat back

C32   The Kames brooch

of the brooch is a talismanic inscription: IHESUS NAZARENUS CRUCIFIXUS REX IUDEORUM IASPER MEL PCHIORA. The back of the pin is engraved with the word ATROPA. The three last names, which are those of two of the Magi and of one of the Fates, in combination with the first part of the inscription, appear in one other ring brooch which was found on Islay, also kept in the National Museum in Edinburgh.

PSAS, xlv (1961–2), 308–9

C33   Silver ornaments from Langhope

Scotland Early 14th century
Part of a hoard of objects which included a number of Edwardian coins found in a three legged brass pot at Langhope, Roxburghshire. Deposited 1318×60
Edinburgh, National Museum NG 25–27

The group includes:
   A wire ring brooch with four rosettes alternating with four knops (60 mm) which show traces of gilding.

C33   Silver ornaments from Langhope

A wire ring brooch with six lozenge shaped plates attached, incised with lines radiating from the centre. The plates show traces of gilding.

A silver finger ring inscribed IEZUS NAZA

PSAS, xvi (1881–2), 244, 407; lviii (1923–4), 168, 173, 174 figs 5: 2 & 3.

C34 Silver ornaments from Dumfries

Scotland Early 14th century
c. 1324×1335
Found in a purse in the wall of an old house in Dumfries along with a number of coins, parts of a chain and a silver hook bow. Deposited *c.* 1324×35.
Edinburgh, National Museum KO 27–31

The group of ornaments comprises:
A complete ring brooch (31 mm).
Parts of two similar brooches decorated with corrugations and niello.
Part of a brooch ornamented with gems set in collets alternating with hemispherical protuberances covered in small pellets (originally 25 mm).
An equal armed cross (35×40 mm) with a loop for suspension, engraved in the central disc with the letters AFLO—the initial letters in Latin characters of a Hebrew inscription meaning 'Thou art mighty for ever O Lord'; nielloed.

PSAS, lviii (1923–4), 160–2.

C35 Two silver brooches from Ayr

Scotland 1292–1360
40 mm
66 mm
Found with coins of Alexander III, John Baliol, and the Edwards in an earthenware pot in the old fort at Ayr in 1892.
Edinburgh, National Museum NG 150–1

One of the brooches is circular. The inscription on the back is a blundered version of the formula IEZUS REX NAZARENUS IVDEORUM. The other brooch is

octagonal in form with a variant of the same talismanic inscription engraved on alternate panels on the back, whilst the front is decorated with a pattern inlaid in niello.

PSAS, xxvi (1891–2), 60; lviii (1923–4), 168, 169, 171, figs 3:12 and 4:2

C36 Hoard of jewelry from Canonbie

Scotland 13th–14th century
From a hoard of valuable things which also included a number of pennies of Edward I and II, John Balliol and Alexander II. Found during the ploughing of a field at Woodhead, Canonbie, Dumfries-shire. Deposited 1298×*c.* 1302
Edinburgh, National Museum KO 3–9

The group of ornaments comprises:
A gold ring set with an irregular shaped pierced sapphire, surrounded by six emerald sparks in individual collets. Pierced gems were believed to have magical properties in medieval times.
A gold ring set with a ruby.
A talismanic ring brooch (54 mm), bearing traces of niello. Inscribed IHESUS NAZARENUS REX.
A wire ring brooch (69 mm) with alternating rosettes and knops.
A half of a wire ring brooch (50 mm) with lozenge-shaped plates attached to the front.
Several small oblong jet beads.

PSAS, v (1826–4), 216; lviii (1923–4), 168, 171, 172, 173, figs 3:1, 5:1 and 4

C37 Gold fillet

Scotland 13th century
330×12 mm
Discovered with four silver gilt spoons under the floor of the Nunnery, Iona.
Edinburgh, National Museum HX 36

The fillet is formed of a thin strip of beaten gold and ornamented with repoussé work in a foliaceous design and has a pellet border. The pattern resembles the embossed scroll work on the silver plate of the Guthrie Bell Shrine.

PSAS, lviii (1923–4), 102, 109

C38 Two rings from Whithorn

Scotland 13th century
Found in two graves excavated at Whithorn Priory near Wigtown, Galloway.
Edinburgh, National Museum

The smaller of the two rings, found in one grave, is silver gilt and has an oblong bezel set with an

C38   Two rings from Whithorn

amethyst.

The other is a gold ring with a large bezel set with an oblong, table cut amethyst surrounded by eight small sapphires in individual collets. The combination of a large gem with a number of subsidiary gems set in this way is typical of the multiple gem ring in the thirteenth century. This ring was found in a grave, where there were also a silver chalice and paten and an enamelled crozier head. The grave was probably that of a bishop. The burial of a bishop with a ring on the hand was traditional in medieval times. A number of rings have been retrieved from bishops' graves of the 12th and 13th centuries. A few have been 'consecration' rings or 'pontificals' but most, like this one, were selected for their decorative rather than official value.

Oman, *British Rings*, nos 16 d, e

C39   Gold brooch
Scotland 14th century
38 mm
Found in the water of Ardoch, near Doune Castle, Perthshire.
Edinburgh, National Museum NGÅ 126

The brooch is made of a piece of twisted gold and is engraved on the front with an inscription in the broad flutings, which begins immediately to the right of the pin hinge. This is in French and reads: +ABEZ DE +MOY MERCIE+ET PITIE MOUN COER EN+BOUS REPOCE (Have mercy and pity on me and let me rest my heart in you).

PSAS, viii (1868–70), 330–333

C40   Gold brooch from Islay
Scotland 14th century
228 mm
From Islay, Argyll.
Edinburgh, National Museum NGA 133

The brooch is engraved with the formula IESUS NAZERENUS R on one side and IASPER MELCHITR ATROP on the other side (representing two of the Magi and one of the Fates).

PSAS, lviii (1923–4), 268, 170.

C41   Two silver spoons
Scotland Late 13th–Early 14th century
Found at Windymains, East Lothian, and in the churchyard in Brechin, Angus, respectively.
Edinburgh, National Museum ME 95 and MEQ 14

The spoons are similar, both having long rounded stems terminating in conical knops and rounded bowls. The spoon found at Brechin (part of a hoard which included coins of Alexander III and Edward I and II) has a slightly shorter stem.

PSAS, lxix (1934–5), 147–8, fig 10; lviii (1923–4), 107, 109

C42   Silver gilt spoons from Iona
Scotland 13th century
c. 200 mm
Found under a stone at the base of the south respond of the chancel arch of the Nunnery at Iona.
Edinburgh, National Museum HX 32–35

The four spoons bear a general similarity to one another, having stems of two parts, the upper portion narrow and rounded terminating in a conical knop, and the lower, flat and broad with ornamentation. Each spoon has a shallow leaf-shaped bowl but only one of these is intact. At the junction of each bowl is a grotesque animal head.

Two of the spoons have exceptionally fine decoration. One of these is distinct from the rest, with a panel of geometric design composed of lozenges enclosing foliaceous figures, inlaid with niello. The other, which appears to have been copied by the craftsman of the remaining two spoons, terminates in a knop which takes the form of a raspberry or mulberry resting in a calyx. The rounded part is notched as if to represent buds on a twig. The flat section of the handle is decorated with a series of groups of concentric curves. The bowl is decorated with incised ornamentation: an elaborate fleur-de-lis or acanthus flower at the top and a line which runs around the edge. The design of the spoons and in particular the pointed shape of the bowl indicate an early date. Features like the grotesque animal heads can also be seen on the thirteenth-century coronation spoon in the Tower of London, which also has a bowl engraved with an acanthus type decoration.

PSAS, lviii (1923–4), 102–9

C43   Bejewelled prick spur

Scotland *c.* 1300
156 mm long
Found in the bed of Loch Monkstadt, Skye, after it was drained in the 1820s.
Edinburgh, National Museum ML (1977)

The spur is made of bronze chased with patterns and floral motifs and shows traces of gilding. There are three sockets on each shank of the spur, one on the prick-stem and two on the point, of which five are still set with stones.

PSAS, iii (1857–60), 103–4

C44   Enamelled hasp

France, Limoges 13th century
350 mm
Found in the bank of Beck's Burn near Wauchope Castle, Langholm, Dumfries-shire.
Edinburgh, National Museum KJ 88

The hasp consists of two parts joined by a hinge, the larger part shaped like a dragon or wyvern with double folded wings and a twisted tail terminating in another dragon head. The other part is in the shape of a dragon coming out of the mouth of another. Both parts are enamelled and gilded.

The hasp was probably originally fitted to a coffer.

PSAS, xxx (1895–96), 7

C42   Silver gilt spoons from Iona

C43   Bejewelled prick spur

C45   Enamelled bronze plaque

France, Limoges Late 12th–13th century
61×61 mm
Found in a grave next to the altar of the Teampull
Bhuirgh (chapel) Borve, Benbecula, Outer
Hebrides.
Edinburgh, National Museum KE (1977)

The plaque is decorated with the figure of Christ, his
head in a cruciform nimbus, his right hand raised in
blessing. At each side is a flower design. Traces of
enamel, now turquoise blue and red, and gilding
remain. Similar plaques have been found in Europe.
The design of this is poor and clumsily contrived.
The plaque originally decorated the centre back of
an altar crucifix, but it has evidently been put to a
different use at a later date; the two holes in the
plaque and the circumstances of its discovery about
the chest of a body in a grave suggests that it was
made into a costume accessory possibly for a
churchman.

PSAS, cix (1977–8), 378–80

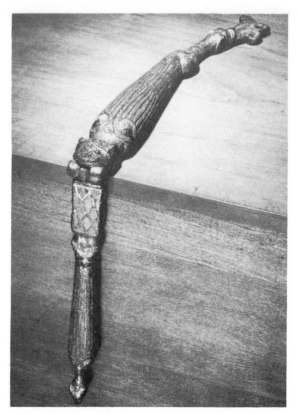

C44   Enamelled hasp

C46   Anthropoid candleholder

C47   Bronze pricket candlestick

France, Limoges 13th century
100×55 mm
From Bothwell Castle, Lanarkshire.
Edinburgh, National Museum HX 506

The pricket candlestick has a hexagonal cast bronze base with a deep sloping flange of six panels each with a fanciful coat of arms. The whole is raised on three plain feet.

C48   Dagger pommel

France, Limoges? Late 14th century
32.5×12.5×27 mm
Edinburgh, National Museum LC (1975–6)

A bronze crescent-shaped dagger-pommel decorated with foliage and coats-of-arms, originally picked out with enamel. The arms, with simple geometric designs, are obviously purely decorative.

PSAS, cvii (1975–6), 322–3

C49   Mould for Pilgrim's badge

Scotland 14th century
73×66 mm
Found in the churchyard of old St Andrew's Church near the harbour of North Berwick, East Lothian.
Edinburgh, National Museum BG 237

The centre part of a stone mould formed of clay-bed ironstone broken at the lower end. On the obverse side are matrices for casting lead or pewter badges.

C46   Anthropoid candleholder

North Europe 14th century
152 mm
From the site of a crannog in the Loch of Leys, Kincardineshire.
Edinburgh, National Museum MGI (1982)

A kneeling figure of a man cast in bronze and originally gilt. One arm is held out and the hand is formed as a loop to contain a spike for a candle. His clothing is decorated with annulets on the shoulders and there is a letter A on his chest—possible the founder's mark.

Although such candleholders are now very rare it is likely that this one is a late example of a series which began with quite an elaborate model. In this case, after a long process of copying one from another, the design has become simplified, concentrating on particularly salient details like the hem of the garment at the left knee.

C47   Bronze pricket candlestick

These show a representation of St Andrew on his cross in an oblong frame with rings at the corners, an equal armed crucifix, and a portion of another. Both these have rings at all the points for the attachment of the badge to the pilgrim's clothing. The reverse has two moulds for ring brooches with thistle-headed pins. Cheap badges or 'signaculi' were produced and sold by tradesmen near to the goal of the pilgrimage or in a town through which pilgrims had to pass. North Berwick was a ferry port for pilgrims travelling to St Andrews.

PSAS, xli (1906–7), 431

C50   Seal matrix of the Cathedral chapter of Brechin

Scotland First half 13th century
69×39 mm
Edinburgh, National Museum NM 11

A brass pointed oval seal matrix. The main field carries a representation of God the Father sitting on a broad bench-like throne and holding in front of him the cross on which God the Son is hanging. PATER is inscribed on the arch enclosing the head of God the Father, and FIL' on the transverse beam of the cross.

The Holy Spirit, in the form of a bird, flies down diagonally between the heads of the Father and the Son. The inscription S' SPS. lies across the shoulder of the Father at the bird's feet. The back of the matrix has a thick, fleshy branched foliate ornament, beginning as a large trefoil, projecting from the mouth of an inverted cat mask, its central stem running the length of the matrix.

Legend: S'. CAPITULI: SANCTE: ×TRINITATIS×D'BRECHIN.

Stevenson & Wood, *Scottish Heraldic Seals*, i, 133

C51   Seal matrix of the chapter of the Church of St Mary, Caithness

Scotland 13th century
83×53 mm
London, British Museum

A pointed oval brass matrix with a handle at the back. It shows a half length figure of the Virgin with the Child under a trefoiled canopy supported on spirally fluted columns. On the dexter side is the head of St Columba, mitred, and on the sinister side the head of St David as a king. Above each is a nimbed angel with outstretched arms. On the upper

C50   Seal matrix of the Cathedral chapter of Brechin

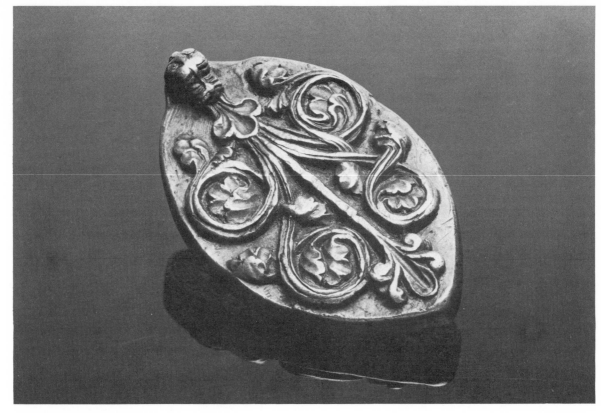

C50 Seal matrix of the Cathedral chapter of Brechin

part of the canopy three niches each contain a bishop's head, while under a trefoiled arch at the base stand nine ecclesiastics holding books.

   Legend: +S' CAPITL'I ECCE SCE GENETRICIS MARIA CATANENSIS.

Tonnochy, *Catalogue of Seal-Dies*, no 936

C52   Seal matrix of the Chapter of the Church of St Magnus, Orkney

Scotland 14th century
73 mm
Edinburgh, National Museum NM 114

A circular brass matrix with beaded borders. There are three canopied niches and, in the centre, on a bracket, stands St Magnus, bareheaded, with sword erect in his right hand. In each of the side niches, on a bracket, kneels a monk with arms raised and extended in adoration towards the saint.

   Legend: SIGILLVM. CAPITVLI. ORKADENSIS. ECCLESIE. SANCTI. MAGNI.

Stevenson & Wood, *Scottish Heraldic Seals*, i, 160

C51   Seal matrix of the chapter of the Church of St Mary, Caithness

C53　Seal matrix of John, Archdeacon of Glasgow

C53　Seal matrix of John, Archdeacon of Glasgow

Scotland 14th century
34×24 mm
Edinburgh, National Museum NM102A

A pointed oval seal matrix with a loop on the back at the top. On a bracket beneath a decorated canopy is a figure of St Kentigern, with mitre, a crozier in his left hand, and his right blessing the Archdeacon, who kneels in front of him on the sinister. Between the figures is the salmon with a ring, associated with St Kentigern, above the archdeacon are two eyes (?) and over the canopy a bird reguardant.

Legend: S'IOH'IS ARCHID' GLASGVEN'

Stevenson & Wood, *Scottish Heraldic Seals*, i, 119

C54　Seal matrix of Inchaffray Abbey

England 14th century
69 mm
London, British Museum

A double sided circular brass seal matrix with three pierced lugs and corresponding pegs. The obverse shows a Gothic church building, with central niche, side towers and pinnacles. Under a canopy in the centre is a nimbed saint with a quill pen and book. The surrounding legend is: + S' COMVNE:ECCE: SCI.IOH'IS:EWANGELISTE.DE.INSVLA.MISSARVM.

The reverse has the same legend surrounding the eagle of St John the Evangelist within a cusped border of eight points. The eagle stands on a scroll which has the legend: I.PRICIPIO:ERAT.VERBV

Tonnochy, *Catalogue of Seal-Dies*, no 938

C55　Seal matrix of the convent of Whithorn, Wigtownshire

Scotland 14th century
50×30 mm
Edinburgh, National Museum NM 147

A brass vesica shaped matrix with the *Agnus Dei*, a chalice beneath its breast.

Legend + S':CONVENTVS: CANDIDE: CASE

Stevenson & Wood, *Scottish Heraldic Seals*, i, 203

C54　Seal matrix of Inchaffray Abbey

C54　Seal matrix of Inchaffray Abbey

C56   Seal matrix of W. Mathew, monk of Arbroath

C56   Seal matrix of W. Matthew, monk of Arbroath

Scotland 13th century
29×22 mm
Edinburgh, National Museum NM29

A small brass, oval matrix with a hexagonal stock and pierced knob. Within a canopied niche resting on a double corbelled bracket stands St Thomas à Becket, front face with mitre, right hand raised in benediction, left holding an archiepiscopal cross, between 2 kneeling angels waving thuribles. Beneath is a half-length figure of a monk kneeling to dexter.

Legend: S. F. W. MATH' I. MONAC'. DABIRBROTHOT.

Stevenson & Wood, *Scottish Heraldic Seals*, i, 169

C57   Seal matrix of a monk of Crossraguel Abbey

Scotland 13th century
33×20 mm
Found in a drain at the Abbey, Ayrshire.
Edinburgh, National Museum NM 201

A leaf shaped, brass seal-matrix. In the upper part is a half-length figure of the Virgin with the Child. Below this a monk in adoration is depicted.

Legend: S. H. MONACHI. DE CARREC.

PSAS, liv (1919–20), 25–26

C58   Seal matrix of the Burgh of Dunblane

Scotland 13th century
59 mm
London, British Museum

The circular bronze seal matrix has a thick handle of hexagonal section at the back. It shows two figures, on the dexter St Lawrence and on the sinister a bishop blessing with a crozier in the left hand, under a pinnacled canopy. St Lawrence holds a book and a gridiron, the symbols of his faith and his martyrdom.

Legend: S' COMUNE BURGI DUNBLANENSIS. This is the only evidence that Dunblane was a burgh at an early date.

Tonnochy, *Catalogue of Seal-Dies*, no 205

C59   Seal matrix of the Burgh of Arbroath

Scotland 13th century
70 mm
Edinburgh, National Museum NM33

A circular lead matrix with a knob on the back. A representation of the martyrdom of St Thomas à Becket. On the dexter are the four conspirators, the one in front with sword raised above the head of the Saint who kneels before the altar, out of which appears a figure holding a chrism in the right hand

C57   Seal matrix of a monk of Crosraguel Abbey   C58   Seal matrix of the Burgh of Dunblane

C59   Seal matrix of the Burgh of Arbroath

and a cross in the left. On the field in chief is an eight-pointed star with a crescent above it, and in base the inverted inscription SANCTUS THMS.

Legend: S' CONVNITATIS BURGI DE ABIRBROTHOT.

The design of the seal is a very crude copy of that on the thirteenth-century seal of Arbroath Abbey. It may be a contemporary forgery.

Stevenson & Wood, *Scottish Heraldic Seals*, i, 53

C60   Seal matrix of Ralph of Coventry

Scotland 13th century
33×21 mm
Found at Culross Abbey, Fife.
Edinburgh, National Museum NM 43

A small, oval, brass matrix with the figure of a bird and bits of foliage.

Legend: S. RADVLFI. DE. COVINTR

C61   Coins, Alexander II—Robert Bruce
Edinburgh, National Museum

Pennies remained the basic unit of currency, half pence and farthings being introduced in the reign of Alexander III. There is much variety in the busts on the coins of Alexander II and the earlier coinage of Alexander III, a few being of considerable merit. A noticeable improvement in quality can be seen in the second coinage of Alexander III, dating from about 1280 and corresponding to the great Edwardian recoinage in England. The few coins of Robert I perhaps owe their neat finish to their value as propaganda pieces.

4 THE ART OF THE WEST HIGHLANDS

By the late fourteenth century it was clear to the Scots and other observers that Scotland contained two nations distinguishable by their different languages, manners and customs. Already the Gaelic speaking people of the West and North were culturally alien from the 'English' speaking Scots settled in the Lowlands. For many of the former their allegiance to the powerful Lords of the Isles came before any ties with the Scottish kings or services due to them. Until their forfeiture in 1493 the Lords of the Isles were frequently at odds with the Scottish kings and for much of the period were no mean rivals for overall power.

It is not surprising that a vigorous and distinctive style of art was fostered in the West Highlands and Isles under these conditions. It is first evident in the fourteenth century and was to survive as late as the eighteenth.

There is little in the way of architecture that marks out the West Highland style, with the exception of the major schemes of construction carried out at the abbey and nunnery on Iona under the patronage of the Lords of the Isles in the second half of the fifteenth century. The work is noted for its rich carving which relates it to the much better known and prolific monumental sculpture—the grave-slabs, effigies and crosses—the most characteristic expressions of the art of the area.

At least four main schools of stone carving, centred on Iona, Oronsay, Kintyre and Lock Awe, have been distinguished. These were not all operating simultaneously, the Iona workshop being earliest in production, by the middle of the fourteenth century. By the beginning of the sixteenth century much of the work was done by individual craftsmen who may have travelled around for work.

In general terms the stone carving is characterised by its overall effect, no significant areas of stone being left bare except on those slabs with high relief effigies of knights and clergy. Early slabs have a cross shaft with floriated head running the length of the stone and a sword at one side, and swords or other symbols of quality or status are a recurring theme.

Even more so is the ubiquitous use of scrolling leaf designs which develop into fantastic animal and dragon heads, often opposed in groups of two. On some stones animals are carved in disassociation from the leaf scrolls, often with great feeling for naturalism, and representing the animals in hunting scenes. Intermixed are unicorns, griffins, dragons and other animals from the bestiaries. Most of the carving is twelfth-century in feel or style and represents a late survival of Romanesque in the West Highlands.

Of great interest is the use of panels of interlace to good effect. Conceivably, this is a deliberate piece of antiquarianism. Its occurrence in West Highland Art may best be seen as a revival rather than the continuation of an older tradition. It is not found on the earlier type of grave-slabs with floriated crosses and swords, and despite its occurrence on the Campbeltown Cross, dated to the late fourteenth century, may not have been generally employed until the mid-fifteenth century.

A few surviving pieces of metalwork indicate that pieces of quality were produced by craftsmen in this area well away from the Lowland burghs. The basic medieval ring brooch was elaborated into a series of prestigious reliquary brooches—the brooch of Lorne, the Lochbuy and Ugadale brooches—with tall collets, silver filigree and large crystals. The Guthrie bell shrine and St Fillan's crozier, both composite works of more than one period but both remodelled in the fifteenth century, give a tantalising glimpse of the treasures of the church in the Highlands. The knop of St Fillan's crozier is decorated with interlace and this was the motif used exclusively to decorate two caskets of whale-bone produced at the turn of the sixteenth century.

A remarkable survival is two West Highland harps or clarsachs, one of which, traditionally known as Queen Mary's, is one of the finest examples of Medieval Art produced in Scotland. It probably dates to about 1450. It is decorated with low relief carvings of foliage and interlace comparable to work on the contemporary stone monuments. The heraldic beasts skilfully lined and set in roundels could be copied straight from a manuscript or copybook, as also perhaps the guilloche and fret designs. The strapwork cross designs on the sounding box and the animal head terminals on the fore-pillar and base of the box hint at a more distant Scoto-Irish ancestry, as does the very instrument itself. The animal head terminals and those on the mounts of the Lamont Harp are the last of a long line going back through St Fillan's crozier, the Kilmichael Glassary bell shrine, St Fillan's bell and even further back to the great penannular brooches of the seventh and eighth centuries and the escutcheons of hanging bowls.

D1 Cross of Reginaldus

Scotland, West Highlands *c.* 1380
1.16×0.465m
From the Island of Texa, off the south coast of Islay.
Edinburgh, National Museum IB 198

Part of a cross-shaft with Reginaldus shown on the front wearing a bascinet (helmet), mail aventail

(protection for the neck and shoulders), and an aketon (quilted protective coat). He has a sword attached to his belt and is grasping an axe. On the back at the base is a galley of West Highland type carrying two people. Above this is a hunting scene depicting two dogs attacking a deer and part of a foliage design. There is an inscription above the figure of Reginaldus, in lombardic capitals unevenly set out, which reads: HEC. E/ST CRU/X REGN/ALDI IO/ H(ANN)IS/DE YSLE
(This is the cross of Reginaldus son of Iohannes of Islay)

This is probably Reginaldus, son of John I, Lord of the Isles who was the eponym of the Clan Ranald. On the death of his elder brother he became heir to the chiefship of the Clan Ruari and to the Lordship of Garmoran, by right of his mother Amy MacRuairi, and his possession was confirmed in January 1373. Although he acted as a 'high steward' over the Isles, he never became 'Lord of the Isles', himself.

Steer and Bannerman, *Medieval Sculpture in the West Highlands*, no 49

D2 Grave slab

Scotland, West Highland 14th or 15th century
1.6×0.53 m
From Kilmory, Knapdale, Argyll.
Edinburgh, National Museum (Cast) IB 232

The head of the stone is decorated with a foliated cross, beneath which is a sword flanked by plant-scrolls of the kind popular at Iona. This stone also carries an inscription on a raised panel on the left side of the sword-hilt and down the blade of the sword. It commemorates three men of the same family who may have been craftsmen in the service of the Lords of the Isles. One of them was a carpenter, and the insignia of his trade, a pair of axes and a block of wood, are carved beside the first part of the epitaph.

The inscription reads 'HIC IACE/'T. IOH(ANN)ES CA/ RPENTARI(VS)/E[T]. FRATRES MOLMORE/ET CRISTINVS. FABER (Here lies Johannes Carpentarius and the brothers Mael-Moire and Cristinus Faber)

Steer and Bannerman, *Medieval Sculpture in the West Highlands*, no 84

D3 Cross shaft and head, Eilean Mor, Knapdale, Argyll

Scotland, West Highlands Probably before 1402
1.52×0.25 m
Formerly stood on the highest point of the island of Eilean Mor.
Edinburgh, National Museum IB 143

D1 Cross of Reginaldus

The cross-head shows the Crucifixion, with two subsidiary figures, one below each of the outstretched arms, and an inscription on a scroll above the Crucifix. This reads I(ESUS) N(AZARENUS) R(EX) I(UDEORUM) (Jesus of Nazareth, King of the Jews). There is also an inscription on the lower part of the shaft, MA[RIO]/TA . DE . R/OS . INSU/LARUM . /DOMIN/A . ET . IO/HANNE/S . PRES/PITER/AC . HER/EMITA I/STE . INS/ULE . ME . /FIERI . F/ECERU/NT (Mariota de Ros, Lady of the Isles, and Iohannes, priest and hermit of this island, caused me to be made). Above this, an ecclesiastical figure is depicted within a niche—possibly the priest mentioned in the inscription. The reverse of the shaft and cross-head is decorated with foliaceous ornament and an animal at the base of the shaft.

This may have been made in the Iona workshop.

Steer and Bannerman, *Medieval Sculpture in the West Highlands*, no 80

D4 Cross

Scotland, West Highland Late 14th century
From Kilchoman churchyard, Islay
2.14×0.52 m
Edinburgh, National Museum IB 217

In the disc-head on the front of the cross is a representation of the crucifix with the rest of the shaft and arms of the cross filled with a design of intertwined leaves issuing from two opposed beasts at the base. The back is covered with a similar foliage design and beasts. The edges of the cross are filled with an inscription which reads: + HEC EST CRVX FAC(TA)PRO ANIMABVS DONCANI MECINNIRLEGIN ET MAR/I ET MICHAELIS (This is the cross made for the souls of Duncanus MacNerlin and Mary MacNerlin and Mary and Michael)

The cross probably dates from the latter half of the fourteenth century. It is likely that the Mary and Michael of the inscription are the Virgin Mary and the Archangel Michael.

Steer and Bannerman, *Medieval Sculpture in the West Highlands*, no 43

D5 Cristin's cross

Scotland, West Highland Second half 15th century
1.85×0.3 m
In the churchyard at Kilkerran, Argyll.
Edinburgh, National Museum (Cast) IB 241

On the front at the top of the shaft an inscription proclaims that HEC/EST/CRUX/CRIS/TINI/M(AC)AYG/ET UX/OR(IS) EI/USS (This is the cross of Cristinus MacKay and his wife). Below this are three niches. The uppermost contains a female figure in an attitude

of prayer, the central one a man and woman embracing, and the lower a warrior on horseback armed with sword and spear, and wearing a helmet resembling a morion. At the base is a casket displaying vertical strapping and a handle. The back of the shaft is decorated with a strip of eight-cord plaitwork at the top, with a double plant-scroll ending in dragons' heads and a galley below it. A number of the designs bear a resemblance to those on Kintyre-type grave-slabs and all these carvings may perhaps have emanated from the same workshop.

Steer and Bannerman, *Medieval Sculpture in the West Highlands*, no 98

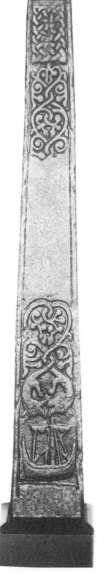

D4   Cross   D5   Cristin's cross

D6 Grave slab, Kilmory, Knapdale, Argyll, of a civilian

D6 Grave slab, Kilmory, Knapdale, Argyll, of a civilian

Scotland, probably from the Iona or Loch Sween Workshops Pre 1500
1.19×0.43 m
From Kilmory, Knapdale, Argyll.
Edinburgh, National Museum (Cast) IB 237

This is the only sizeable late medieval effigy of a civilian in the West Highlands. The figure is attired in a knee-length pleated tunic belted at the waist; it has puffed sleeves with narrow cuffs, and traces of herringbone pattern are visible on the hem. A separate garment, indented along both the top and bottom edges, covers his neck and shoulders. He also wears a Burgundian hat. A badly worn inscription tells us that the man's forename was John: +HI[C] AC[ET]/ IO[HA(N)N]/ES . . (Here lies John . . . . . .). He was probably a prominent member of the group of craftsmen at Kilmory who may have enjoyed a special position as direct employees of the Lords of the Isles.

Steer and Bannerman, *Medieval Sculpture in the West Highlands*, no 83

D7 Head of free standing cross

Scotland, West Highland Early 16th century
0.81×0.61 m
Found at Taynuilt, Lorn, Argyll.
Edinburgh, National Museum IB 134

This disc-headed cross is carved of slate and has a figure of the crucified Christ, the body slumped, the legs bent sideways. The attitude of the Saviour here may be compared with that on the Lerags Cross also in Lorn, the two being identical except for the position of the head. On both these crosses the figure has been given added emphasis by cutting a deep hollow round it. Both are probably the work of the same carver.

Steer and Bannerman, *Medieval Sculpture in the West Highlands*, p 76

D8 Tomb of Alexander Macleod of Dunvegan

Scotland, West Highland 1528
In the south wall of the choir of St Clement's Church, Rodel, Harris, Outer Hebrides.
Edinburgh, National Museum (cast and photographic assemblage)

Wall-tombs are rare in the West Highlands, having been introduced *c.* 1500. Of the earlier ones, that of Alexander MacLeod is the most remarkable. The effigy, dressed in plate armour with a bascinet and aventail, rests on a stone coffin which projects slightly into the body of the church, and is covered by a semi-circular recessed arch. The voussoirs of the arch are elaborately carved with representations of the Holy Trinity surrounded by the Evangelist symbols, angels holding censers, and the Twelve Apostles, grouped in pairs. This is the first known appearance of the Twelve Apostles on late medieval West Highland sculpture.

The decoration at the back of the recess is dominated by three panels containing canopied figures of the Virgin and Child flanked on the right by St Clement, and on the left by an unnamed bishop. This central row of panels is completed with carvings of a galley and a castle, which were the emblems of the MacLeods. The row above displays a blazing sun of twelve rays surrounded by angels carrying candles, and blowing trumpets. The bottom row encompasses the main inscription, a representation of St Michael and Satan at the weighing of the souls, and a hunting scene with Alexander MacLeod attended by two gillies.

This wealth of sculpture is without parallel on any Scottish wall-tomb.

The main inscription reads:
hic.localus.co(m)posuit/p(er) d(omi)n(u)m. allexo(n)der.filius.vil(el)mi/mac.clod.d(omi)no.de du(n)began/anno. d(omi)ni.m°.ccccc°.xxviii° (This tomb was prepared by Lord Alexander, son of Willelmus MacLeod, Lord of Dunvegan, in the year of Our Lord 1528).

Steer and Bannerman, *Medieval Sculpture in the West Highlands*, no 2

D9   Grave slab

Scotland, West Highlands *c.* 1500–1560
From Texa, Islay.
Edinburgh, National Museum IB 199

D9   Grave slab

Unfortunately the grave-slab is considerably damaged, but a figure in clerical dress is still visible. From what remains of the inscription, this figure is identified as John MacAlister, parson of Gigha. . . . [iohann]es.ioha(nn)is.m(ac)alistaire.re[ctor/ de. . . . . .m]aur/icius. macaeda. vicar[i]us.eidem . . . . . (. . .Iohannes, son of Iohannes MacAlister, parson of . . . . Mauricius MacKay, vicar of the same, ...)

Steer and Bannerman, *Medieval Sculpture in the West Highlands*, no 50

D10   Grave slab of Murchardus Macduffie of Colonsay

Scotland, West Highland (Oronsay School) 1539
1.70×0.48 m
Oronsay Priory, Argyll
Edinburgh, National Museum (Cast) IB 141

This is one of the most elegant of all the West Highland grave-slabs. The central space is occupied by a claymore, above which is a representation of a deer-hunt. On either side of the blade are plant-scrolls, which are terminated immediately below the swordguard with a griffin and another mythical beast. At the base of the slab is a representation of a galley. The plant-scroll, galley and claymore are typical of the Oronsay school. The decoration has borders on three sides, two of which contain an inscription which reads: hic iacet murchardus macdufie de co (llonsa qui ob)iit a(n)no do(mini) m°d°xxx°ix° et mari/ota nicilleain me fi(eri fecit) (here lies Murchardus MacDuffie of Colonsay who died in the year of our Lord 1539; and Mariota MacLean caused me to be made).
Steer and Bannerman, *Medieval Sculpture in the West Highlands*, no 35

D11   The Dunvegan cup

Ireland 1493
0.25×0.13 m
Long in the possession of the MacLeods of Dunvegan, Skye.
Dunvegan Castle, Skye

The cup is a type of Irish drinking vessel known as a mether. It is made of wood, stands on four legs with feet like shoes, has an ornamental ledge and is covered with mountings of silver with niello and gilding and settings for precious stones, which include four large sockets for gems at the four corners of the ledge. The plaques on the cup comprise two types of ornament: filigree work and a sort of pierced work which is imitative of Gothic tracery. The mouth of the vessel is formed of a broad four-sided silver rim on which is engraved an inscription which reads: Katharina nigen uy Neill uxor iohannis megvigir principis de firmanac me fieri fecit anno domini 1493. oculi omnium in te sperant domine et tu daz escam illorum in tempore

D10 Grave slab of Murchardus Macduffie of Colonsay

D11 The Dunvegan cup

opportuno.

The last part of the inscription is part of verse 15 of Psalm 144. It is not certain who exactly are referred to by the names on the cup. John son of the MacGuire may be the same person whose name appears in The Annals of the Four Masters in 1484 and may have been married to 'Katherina'.

It is probable that the cup is older than the inscription. It is not known how it came into the possession of the Dunvegan family.

PSAS, xlvii (1912–13), 102–9

D12 The quigrich—St Fillan's crozier

Scotland 14th–15th century
230×200 mm
Kept at Eyich near Crianlarich for several centuries, by the hereditary guardians of the Shrine, the Dewars of Glendochart.
Edinburgh, National Museum KC 1

The Shrine is silver gilt and made as a 'crook' ornamented with filigree plaques fixed into spaces between a network of raised engraved metal. Plaques from the earlier shrine which this enclosed were transferred to it and are detectable because of a slight difference in execution. The crozier end is similarly ornamented and has a setting with a crystal. At the top is a representation of the head and shoulders of a man, probably meant to be St. Fillan. The knop is decorated with panels of triquetra interlace. The whole shrine has a ridge engraved and pierced with a row of quatrefoil perforations.

On the terminal plate of the crook end is an engraving of a crucifixion flanked by two stars,

D12   The Quigrich—St Fillan's crozier

D13   The Guthrie bell shrine

which is thought to have been added at the end of the fifteenth or beginning of the sixteenth century. The stars may represent the house of Murray—John Murray was Prior of Strathfillan at this time.

In shape and general appearance the shrine resembles some medieval Irish staff reliquaries but the details of its decoration, however, are not typical of Irish art or workmanship. It is possible that the whole (outer) Shrine dates from the period ascribed to the engraving of the crucifixion on the terminal plate and not as has otherwise been suggested, to the fourteenth century.

PSAS, xii (1876–8), 122–82

D13   The Guthrie bell shrine

Scotland, West Highland. A composite object dating from the 12th century or earlier with alteration and additions of later date.
140×112×210 mm
Preserved for many years at Guthrie Castle, Angus.
Edinburgh, National Museum KA 21

The shrine is modelled round an iron quadrangular hand-bell of early date. Bronze plates and an embossed silver plate on the front, with foliage designs outlining a cross with a gilt bronze figure of Christ, have been rivetted on to it. A small figure of St John, now on the side of the bell, and a now missing St Mary and a 'Manus Dei' would have completed this fine 12th-century composition.

At a later date a silver-gilt figure of God the Father and two silver bishops have been added to the front and a bronze bishop to one of the sides. These date to the late 13th or the first half of the 14th century and probably originally belonged to another West Highland shrine. The front is also decorated with two silver-gilt circular settings of gemstones but only the collets remain.

A silver inscription plate fixed upside down below the crucifix states that Iohannes Alexandri me fieri feisit (John the son of Alexander commissioned me to be made).

This may have been John II, Lord of the Isles, whose father was Alexander, and relates to a late fifteenth- or early sixteenth-century remodelling.

PSAS, lx (1925–6), 409–20; Steer and Bannerman, *Medieval Sculpture in the West Highlands*, 29–30, 100, 145.

D14   Octagonal silver brooch

Scotland, West Highland 15th century
86 mm
Found on Mull
Edinburgh, National Museum NGA 116

The sides of the brooch are concave and divided front and back into panels with designs reserved alternatively against niello and cross-hatching. On the front the panels with niello have 'anan' once and 'ihcn' repeated three times in black letter (for IHESUS NAZARENUS), and the other panels have foliage and flower heads or lozenges. On the reverse, zoomorphic designs replace the formulae, alternating with floral motifs.

PSAS, xvii (1882–3), 76–78

D15   The Lochbuy brooch

Scotland, West Highland *c.* 1500
121 ×68 mm
Previously belonged to the MacLeans of Lochbuy in Mull.
London, British Museum

The brooch is of silver gilt, decorated with small bosses and filigree work and has ten turrets 25 mm high set with river pearls. At the centre is a sealed decafoil capsule set with a large crystal.

The Lochbuy Brooch compares closely with two others of West Highland workmanship. Probably the earliest of the three is the Brooch of Lorne, perhaps dating to the mid fifteenth century. It is the prototype of the Lochbuy Brooch, and its capsule unscrews to reveal a cavity for housing a relic or keepsake.

D16   The Ugadale, or Lossit, brooch

Scotland, West Highland Early 16th century
250 mm
Edinburgh, National Museum NGD 11 (replica)

The brooch is silver gilt and has an outer band decorated with strap-work. Within it, eight turrets set with coral and pearls alternate with small round bosses. The oval, ridged crystal in the middle is set on the lid of a capsule ornamented with filigree, which opens to reveal a relic container.

According to tradition the brooch was given to the Mackays by Robert Bruce after he stayed at Ugadale, but at least in its present form, is considerably later than Bruce's time.

D17   Whalebone casket

Scotland 15th or Early 16th century
260×110×120 mm
Formerly preserved at Eglinton Castle in Ayrshire.
Edinburgh, National Museum UD 10

The casket is formed of six plates of bone dovetailed together and strengthened on the corners by vertical angle plates of bronze held in place by horizontal

D14 Octagonal silver brooch

D15 The Lochbuy brooch

straps. The top, bottom, back and front of the box each have four transverse metal straps. The front has a lock, with a double hasp. The bone plates are carved in individual panels between the straps, with interlaced patterns. The bottom has two large squares of interlaced knotwork with a rectangular plaited pattern in the centre. The panels on the casket vary in design from one to another. Only the lid has repeated patterns, one of which (the six cord plait) is also carved on the back and bottom of the casket. This type of decoration is also found on medieval cross slabs in the Highlands of Scotland.

It is thought that such caskets may once have been common in the West Highlands of Scotland for similar caskets can be seen on certain grave slabs, for example, from Iona and Mull and a cross from Kilkerran near Campbelltown.

PSAS, lx (1925–6), 105–17

D18 Whalebone casket

Scotland, West Highland 15th–Early 16th century
220×130×110 mm
Said to come from Fife.
Edinburgh, National Museum L.1949.2

The casket closely resembles the example from Eglinton. It is formed of six bone plates secured

D17 Whalebone casket

together by metal mountings and has similar metal straps strengthening all sides, between which the bone is carved into panels of interlace. The designs on the Fife casket are also varied but there is a greater repetition in the pattern. Three of them appear also on the Eglinton casket.

PSAS, lx (1925–6), 110–17

D19 Tableman from Rhum

Scotland, West Highland 16th century
48 mm
Found in a cave on the east side of the Island of Rhum, Inverness-shire.
Edinburgh, National Museum NS 92

A playing-piece made of cetacean bone, ornamented on one side with a carved interlace design.

PSAS, lxxviii (1943–4), 139

D20 Bone playing-piece

Scotland 15th–16th century
31 mm
From Urquhart Castle, Inverness-shire.
Edinburgh, National Museum HY22

Carved with a design of a horseman with an animal, like a rabbit, in the background.

D21 Whalebone playing-piece

Scotland 15th–16th century
38 mm
Found at Iona Abbey, in the room north of the chapterhouse.
Edinburgh, National Museum NS 99

A tableman carved with a crowned mermaid holding a fish and her own tail.

PSAS, lxxxvii (1952–3), 203

D22 The Queen Mary harp

Scotland *c.* 1450
0.812×0.51 m

Said to have been given to Beatrix Gardyn of Banchory by Mary Queen of Scots. For a long time in the possession of the Robertsons of Lude in Perthshire and subsequently John Stewart of Dalguise.
Edinburgh, National Museum LT 1

The finest of the surviving medieval clarsachs in Scotland. It is made of hornbeam wood, and is highly decorated with low relief carving, shallow tooling and fine engraving, emphasised by a black inlay and staining. The triangular sounding-box which is carved out of a solid block of wood bears bold geometric patterns, and the projecting foot is carved into an animal's head.

The forepillar has a broad central grip carved with a reptile-like head at either end, with 'manes' of interlaced straps and palmettes, which recall motifs on West Highland slabs. A row of silver studs is inserted along the centre of the grip. The sides of the pillar are decorated with a foliaceous pattern with leaf scrolls and palmettes and four roundels containing different animals: griffins, a dragon, a

D23 The Lamont harp

D22   The Queen Mary harp

horse, a dog and a fish.

The harmonic curve, with a hump characteristic of the Scottish highland harp, has geometric decorations along the sides. The three main parts of the instrument, which are socketed into one another, are meant to be held together by the tension of the strings alone. Of the latter there were 30 including an additional bass string.

The Queen May Harp closely resembles another medieval harp in Trinity College, Dublin.

Armstrong, *The Irish and the Highland Harps*, 168–83

D23   The Lamont harp

Scotland *c*. 1500
0.952×0.469 m
Preserved by the Robertsons of Lude in Perthshire for several generations before passing to John Stewart of Dalguise.
Edinburgh, National Museum LT 2

In this second surviving Scottish clarsach, the decoration is almost completely restricted to the brass fittings, the finely crafted string guards on the string band, the straps securing the harmonic curve to the forepillar which terminate in dragon-heads, and the brass enrichment on the end of the harmonic curve, which has a representation of a crystal cabochon in brass on the front, surrounded by foliaceous patterns engraved above and below.

The forepillar has a prominent flat-faced grip on which a circle has been engraved. This clarsach is constructed in a similar manner to the 'Queen Mary' harp with the three main wooden parts socketed with one another. However, the design has been less successful in coping with the extreme tension of the strings, and has suffered bad distortion of the harmonic curve and a succession of fractures in the forepillar, for which reason the metal straps were applied at top and bottom.

The harp originally had 32 strings.

Armstrong, *The Irish and the Highland Harps*, 159–68

5   LATE MEDIEVAL ART

In the later fourteenth century Scotland was cursed by long periods of weak government—a long minority, a king held in English captivity and ageing and ineffective rulers. The wars with England brought misery and desolation and there were outbreaks of plague and famine. All this is reflected in the lack of ambitious building projects at this time.

Despite such adverse conditions the burghs managed to thrive and expand and the burgesses, thanks to their wealth, founded on trade and commerce, became a power to be reckoned with. Their interest in the arts and learning increased and various craft skills were developed.

All this is more evident in the more stable conditions that characterised much of the fifteenth century.

In the first half of the century Scotland's first two universities, St Andrews and Glasgow, were founded. A new wave of church building as well as a growth in secular buildings such as castles, palaces and halls followed the almost total dearth of construction in the century before. The burghs made their own significant contributions in the erection of churches like St Michael's, Linlithgow, the Church of Holyrood at Stirling and St John's Kirk, Perth. Also for the first time in substantial numbers, laymen were founding churches, chapels

Kings College, Aberdeen University—the late 15th century tower with crown steeple

St Michael's Church, Linlithgow—the apse

St Michael's Church, Linlithgow—view of porch and south aisle

and chantries. The sumptuously decorated Roslin Chapel founded by Sir William Sinclair around 1450 is perhaps the finest example.

During the fifteenth and sixteenth centuries trade and other communications with Europe and in particular Flanders and France ensured that a great deal of artistic material either emanated from these countries, or was influenced by their artistic traditions.

There is strong evidence of continental influence in many Scottish churches of the period, and it is likely that French and Flemish masons and architects had a hand in several projects. The influence of English architecture which had dominated in the twelfth and thirteenth centuries declined, though it is still perceptible in the general design and details of Melrose Abbey, reconstructed from 1389 onwards, and in Sweetheart Abbey. At Melrose there are also, however, distinctly 'French' elements like the complex flying buttresses and some windows, dating from the later phases of the reconstruction. French influence has been detected in many other later Gothic churches in Scotland, particularly in window tracery, for example Lincluden Collegiate Church and Paisley Abbey where there are traceried windows resembling those at Melrose. At St Michael's Church, Linlithgow, the window of the south transept contains a simple type of French flamboyant style tracery.

There are also examples of Flemish influence in Scottish architecture in this period, especially among the burgh churches. The church of St Mary's at Haddington, for instance, closely resembles both in detail and general appearance the churches of St Bavo in Harlem and the New Orleans church at Amsterdam.

Further evidence of a general change in Scotland's orientation away from England and towards the Continent in architecture is found in the adoption of certain architectural modes which were contemporary in Europe but unusual or in decline in England. One example is the use of the polygonal apse, a feature found at Crossraguel Abbey and King's College Chapel, Aberdeen, which was not common in England but is often found on the Continent in the fifteenth century. The exceptional Roslin chapel, which with its fantastic sculptural decoration is difficult to place in Scottish tradition, has variously been thought to have been influenced by Iberian architecture and churches in the north east of France, for example St Esprit at Rue on the Picardy coast and a church in the Champagne region.

Continental influences in the fifteenth century however did not entirely dominate Scottish architecture. Unlike the twelfth century when English Romanesque seems to have been transplanted into Scotland there was no wholesale adoption of French or other contemporary architectural idioms. In fact with the decline of English influence, Scotland had begun to develop her own native tradition, and for the first time Scottish churches can be said to be truly Scottish in character. Foreign elements, though strongly in evidence, must be seen as superficial intrusions and not signs of blanket imitation. Scottish architecture was quite independently embarking on a new trend characterised by a return to earlier modes of the Romanesque and transitional styles in which preference was given to lower buildings, heavier piers and thicker walls. Experiments with rib vaulting were on the whole given up in favour of tunnel vaulting with an arch-pointed profile sometimes with applied surface ribs. The evidence suggests that outside sources occasionally provided suitable models for the realization of this tendency in individual cases. The appearance of cylindrical piers at Dunkeld Cathedral, for example, which was begun in 1406, may be connected with the use of such piers in churches in Brabant, like the contemporary Notre Dame de la Chapelle, but in most cases the foreign model was adapted, and not merely copied, and contributed to rather than dominated the indigenous architecture.

In manuscript art on the other hand continental influences were more thorough going.

Many of the manuscripts with Scottish provenances which survive from the fifteenth and sixteenth centuries were imported. Some were specially commissioned by private patrons, among the aristocracy and clergy, and by royalty. Most of them were books of hours or other devotional books, and psalters with a high degree of good quality illumination. Many of the original owners are known to us by name. The book of hours of James IV and Margaret Tudor written in Flanders and illuminated by artists in the Ghent/Bruges School of illumination is probably the most famous. There were also books of secular interest such as the copy of the works of Virgil which came from France and has fine miniatures and historiated initials in a style imitative of William Vrelant.

The demand for imported books must have been high and a number of the incoming products were evidently made for both the Scottish as well as English markets. These books are characterised by adaptations or additions for Scottish use like the special inclusion of devotions to Scottish saints. One book adapted in this way is a book of hours made in France, now in the British Library (Add 39761) which has two extra gatherings of leaves comprising a suffrage to Queen Margaret and devotions to St George and St Ninian, probably made for a Scottish lady. In some foreign books a representation of the Royal Arms of Scotland has been added, for example in the border decoration to Psalm 1 in the fifteenth-century Psalter and Hours from Aberdeen (NLS Adv. 18.8.14).

The decoration of the incoming Flemish manuscripts was particularly influential in Scotland, though not always imitated with success. The low quality of some of the manuscripts which survive,

however, is not always an indication of Scottish workmanship, but may equally point to low grade continental production. Among the better quality Scottish manuscripts made at the end of the fifteenth century, are the three Arbuthnott books which have fine borders decorated with almost naturalistic flowers linked by (pen drawn) scrolls, closely related to the border decoration of early Flemish books such as the Perth Psalter. The Lundy Hours and the Kinloss or Boswell Psalter reflect the subsequent naturalistic phase in Flemish Art and have borders painted with realistic—even recognisable flowers.

Several secular manuscripts which were written and decorated in Scotland have also come down to us. These include many chronicles, university texts and ecclesiastical registers or inventories. In most cases the decoration is limited and not very skilful but there are good examples like the Scotichronicon in Corpus Christi College, Cambridge, which has several lively ink-drawn illustrations of historical scenes. There is also the beautifully ornamented document confirming the marriage treaty between James IV and Margaret Tudor, illuminated by sir Thomas Galbraith, clerk of the Chapel Royal at Stirling.

From the middle of the fifteenth century onward manuscript illumination began to be undermined by the production of printed books, though in the early stages printed books were sometimes ornamented by hand. The art of illumination was increasingly reserved for books where a look of luxury was desired, specialised books, or books which were uneconomical to print. After the Reformation, of course, certain types of religious books ceased to be made and decoration of ecclesiastical manuscripts was discouraged.

Fifteenth- and sixteenth-century metalwork and woodwork in Scotland similarly reflects trading and cultural links with the Continent. A great deal of domestic and ecclesiastical furnishings including jewelry, plate and textiles besides books was imported from Flanders for general consumption by the burgesses. Many items were specially commissioned by wealthy individuals, churchmen and nobles, such as the Trinity Church altarpiece painted by Hugo van der Goes in the 1470s. There is also evidence to suggest that a variety of different Flemish craftsmen were living and working in Scotland. John Fendour who was commissioned by the Burgh of Aberdeen to make the choir stalls for St Nicholas Church early in the sixteenth century, for example, may have come from Flanders.

Scottish crafts were not submerged by the importation of foreign goods and craftsmen. On the contrary, in this period of increasing wealth in Scotland they were able to flourish alongside such imports. Inevitably, there was considerable cross-fertilisation of Scottish with European traditions and it is sometimes difficult to distinguish between native and foreign workmanship. From the style of some of the surviving carved wooden panels and brass furnishings, such as the Beaton panels, and the brass lectern from Holyrood Abbey we do not know for sure whether they were made in Flanders or in Scotland.

Some skills, however, were specifically sought abroad. Maces of the Faculty of Arts of St Andrews University, of the College of St Salvators and the Mace of the University of Glasgow, were all made by French goldsmiths. These display a degree of highly-skilled craftsmanship which perhaps was not available at the time in Scotland, although the Mace of the Faculty of Canon Law of St Andrews, which is modelled closely on the earlier Mace of the Faculty of Arts, seems indeed to be Scottish.

On the other hand, the skill of at least some Scottish metalworkers is reflected in the coinage of the period, particularly the beautifully designed riders and unicorns of James III. The 'true' portraits which first appear on his coinage are considerably in advance of anything elsewhere, except in Italy, the three-quarter facing bust on the groats produced in the 1480s being particularly fine.

E1 Trinity College, Edinburgh, architectural fragments

Scotland Late 15th century
Edinburgh, National Museum KG 105, 108

Trinity College Church, situated on the southwest shoulder of Calton Hill, was founded in 1460 by Marie of Guilders in memory of her husband James II. The church was composed of an apse, a chancel three bays long with side aisles, and a short transept. Work was discontinued in 1531 before the nave could be built. In 1848 the church was demolished to make way for Waverley Station and in 1872, after having lain exposed on Calton Hill for nearly 30 years, some of its stones were incorporated into a new church dedicated to the Holy Trinity built on Jeffrey Street.

Edinburgh Inv, no 4

Three capitals

Scotland Late 15th century
0.20×0.31×0.24 m
0.37×0.34×0.45 m
0.28×0.35×0.39 m

Three capitals from Trinity College Church, deeply carved on 3 sides with stiff-leaf foliage. The design of the foliage varies considerably and on one capital pine cones are included. The capitals would all have carried the ribs of the tierceron vaulting of the chancel. In turn they rested upon slender wall shafts which issued from carved corbels situated in the spandrels of the chancel arcade.

E2 Lintel with the royal arms

Scotland Late 15th century
1.07×0.42×0.23 m
Found in Leith.
Edinburgh, National Museum IB 180

A lintel carved with the Royal Arms of Scotland borne by two supporters. The absence of the portion of the double tressure above the lion rampant indicates that this sculpture dates from after 1471. An Act of Parliament of February 1471 stated that 'The King (James III) with the advice of the three Estates ordained that in time to come there should be no double tressure about his arms but that he should bear whole arms of the lyoun without any more'. In actual fact the double tressure never completely left the arms, but as may be seen here, was retained on the two sides of the lion. The manner in which these terminate here suggests a date soon after the Act, probably the 1470s or early 1480s. The lintel comes from Leith, perhaps from the King's Work, a royal property used as a warehouse.

E3 Lintel of aumbry

Scotland 15th century
0.64×0.37×0.11 m
From Edward Hope's House, Todd's Close, Castle Hill, Edinburgh.
Edinburgh, National Museum KG 37

The top of an aumbry with ogee arch, decoratively cusped.

E4 Boss with figures

Scotland Late 15th century
0.37×0.32 m
From Roslin Collegiate Church, Midlothian.
Edinburgh, National Museum KG 81 (cast)

This cast is of the boss in the second chapel from the

north. On one side are the Virgin and Child, enthroned. To her left are three emaciated figures holding staves, and next to them are three robed and seated men holding sceptres or batons and apparently crowned. To the right of the Virgin is what appears to be a trestle table on which stand three chalices or cups.

The scene has been variously interpreted as representing 'the Dance of Death', or else the three dead and the three living Kings, a homily on the vanity of moral greatness. It is perhaps more likely to be an Adoration with the three shepherds and three wise men.

E5 Tomb front

Scotland 1425–1450
1.46×0.51 m
From the Abbey Church, Coupar Angus.
Edinburgh, National Museum (cast)

The tomb front is divided into six niches with ogee crocketed arches, each of which contains a small figure carved in relief. Two of these are knights in armour, two dressed in long garments and caps are certainly civilians, possibly burgesses or merchants, and the figure in the extreme right-hand niche is probably an infantryman.

The general design of the tomb front is not unusual among medieval tombs in Scotland but the detail of the carved figures makes it one of the most interesting of surviving examples.

E6 Tomb front

Scotland *c.* 1440–60
Renfrew Parish Church
Edinburgh, National Museum (cast)

The tomb front has nine coats-of-arms, all supported by angels, and there are two angel musicians at the ends. It comes from a monument containing the supposed effigies of Sir John Ross of Hawkhead and his wife Marjory Muir.

PSAS, xxiv (1894–5), 368–74

E7 Effigies of a knight and lady

Scotland 1440–1460
From a tomb in the aisle of the old church at Houston, Renfrewshire; now in the nave of the modern church.
Edinburgh, National Museum (casts)

The effigies are life-size and thought to be Sir Patrick Houston who died in 1440 and his wife, Agnes Campbell, who died in 1456.

The knight is depicted with plate defences on his arms and legs and a bascinet (helmet) with its visor removed. His face has been remodelled in a recent restoration. Protecting his body he has a mail habergeon with a breast plate and coat-armour over it, decorated with his coat-of-arms. His sword and dagger have been broken off but his feet still rest on a miniature lion grasping a lamb in its claws.

The lady wears a long cloak, or mantle, tied at her neck with a cord and decorated with embroidered(?) borders. Underneath she has a sideless gown, also with embroidered edges, and beneath that a kirtle fastened with a belt round the waist. Her head is covered with a veil held in place by a padded roll. Her face has suffered from some recent remodelling.

PSAS, xxix (1894–5), 396, 398

E6   Tomb front

E5   Tomb front

E7   Effiges of a knight and lady

E8 Effigy of a mason

E8 Effigy of a mason

Scotland Late 14th–Early 15th century
0.954×0.463 m
Found in the wall of the north east tower of the
Abbey wall, St Andrews.
Scottish Development Department

This recumbent effigy shows a master mason with
his hands in the attitude of prayer. He is dressed in a
gown and hood, his head resting on two tasselled
cushions, and his feet on a mason's mallet. To the
right of the figure lies a hammer, and to the left a
mason's square.

PSAS, lxix (1914–15), 221–2, fig 9

E9 Effigy of a bishop

Scotland 1400–50
1.384 m
Arbroath Abbey
Edinburgh, National Museum (cast)

This effigy, although lacking its head, is of interest
on account of the state of preservation of some of the
details of the costume, particularly the abundance of
jewels and pearls on the orphrey. It has not been
possible to identify who the carving commemorates.

PSAS, xxix (1894–5), 339

E10 Statue of a bishop

Scotland 15th century
0.67×0.42×0.235 m
From Newbattle Abbey, Midlothian.
Edinburgh, National Museum L.1950.18

A seated figure of a bishop, now lacking its head. He
clasps a book in his left hand and the right may have
been outstretched in blessing.

Midlothian Inv, p 144

E11 Statue of St John the Baptist

Scotland (?) 16th century (?)
0.343 m high
Dredged up in the Firth of Forth.
Edinburgh, National Museum KG 6

This limestone statue is of John the Baptist. He is
represented by the symbols of a lamb and cross on a
book which he holds in his left hand. Here he is
portrayed as meagre and wasted, with unshorn beard
and hair, in the rough clothes of a wandering
evangelist. The figure is hollowed at the back with a
hole cut upwards at the bottom as if for setting
upright on a peg.

St John the Baptist was a popular saint and many
churches in Scotland were dedicated to him.

PSAS, vii (1868–8), 397

E10 Statue of a bishop

E12 Stone statuette of St Eloi (St Giles)

Scotland 15th century
0.66×0.23×0.17 m
Found under the floor of the parish church at Rutherglen.
Rutherglen Museum, Glasgow

A statuette of St Eloi, also called St Giles, a Bishop of Noyon in France, who was adopted in Scotland as the patron saint of the Hammermen. The figure is dressed in bishop's clothing. He holds a crozier in his left hand and a hammer with a crown over it, the symbol of the Hammermen, in his right.

E13 Fragment of retable

Scotland Late 15th century
279×254 mm
From Paisley Abbey, Renfrewshire.
Edinburgh, National Museum KG 111 (cast)

The original is carved in sandstone and forms part of

two scenes from the Passion. To the left is the Crucifixion and Christ's legs, nailed one on top of the other, and the Centurion, in plate armour with a long mantle both survive. On the right is the Entombment with a naked Christ laid on a shroud resting on a tomb. Beneath both scenes is the coat-of-arms of Prior George Shaw (1472–98) and part of an inscription.

PSAS, lxii (1927–8), 208–9

E11 Statue of St John the Baptist

E12   Stone statuette of St Eloi (St Giles)

E14   Alabaster panel

Flemish? Early 16th century
120×130 mm
Found in the Pleasance, Edinburgh.
Edinburgh, National Museum KG 5

The panel portrays Christ before Pilate and may be from a set of carvings telling the story of the Passion, forming a small retable behind the altar of a private chapel.

E15   Fragment of a carved stone retable

Scotland 15th century
0.584×0.635 m
Found among building stones when clearing the foundations of a house in Mary King's Close off the High Street, Edinburgh, in 1859.
Edinburgh, National Museum KG 35

The carving, which represents 'Extreme Unction', would have belonged to a group of retable panels portraying the seven sacraments. A figure lying on his death bed is surrounded by a number of clerics preparing to administer the Sacraments of Communion and Extreme Unction. Interesting details in the carving include a table with a collection of ewers and a loaf of bread, and a chamber pot under the bed.

PSAS, lxii (1927–8), 206

E16   Stone carving of the flagellation

Scotland Late 15th century
0.457×0.445 m
From Haddington, East Lothian.
Edinburgh, National Museum L.1950.19

Christ is shown centrally beneath a canopy. Both hands are tied to a pillar behind his head and his naked body is being lashed by two soldiers on either side. The carving probably formed part of a retable depicting the Passion, and this scene of the Flagellation framed a window. It may have come from St Mary's Church in Haddington.

E17   Wooden figure

Scotland Late 15th–Early 16th century
0.457×0.292 m
From West Lothian.
Edinburgh, National Museum

A figure thought to be St Joseph or St Luke, opening the lid of a desk in front of him beneath which are the heads of two animals, possibly an ox and an ass. The figure wears a fur hat and a long belted robe with a tippet covering the shoulders.

PSAS, lx (1925–6), 388, fig 2.

E14   Alabaster panel

E18   Carved oak bishop

Scotland 15th century
0.825 m
Found in a moss near Whithorn Priory.
Edinburgh, National Museum

The figure is blackened by peat in which it has been
immersed for a long time. It is vested in chasuble and
mitre. The arms, which were not carved out of the
block but inserted into holes in the figure, probably
extended outwards, with one hand making the sign
of the blessing and the other holding a crozier.

PSAS, xxxiv (1899–1900), 41, 42

E19   Oak statue of St Andrew

Low Countries? *c.* 1500
From Fife.
Edinburgh, National Museum

A statue of St Andrew carrying his cross, dressed in
long robes and holding a book in a pouch in his right
hand. It has been hollowed out, probably to make it
lighter. The narrow opening at the back is covered
by a panel of wood nailed in. Made to be seen from
three sides only, it probably formed part of a screen.

E20   Wooden panel with Virgin and Child

Scotland Early 16th century
Said to have come from Mary of Guise's House,
Blyth's Close, Castle Hill, Edinburgh.
Edinburgh, National Museum

The figures of the Virgin and Child are set in a round
headed recess framed by panels of Gothic pierced
fenestration set at an angle and surmounted by
acanthus ornamented capitals. On either side of
these are two straps carved with a similar design
containing a shallow niche with a head of shell
formation surmounted by a crocketted canopy. The
whole is supported on a richly ornamented plinth,
the base of which has a range of Gothic pointed
arches.

E15   Fragment of a carved stone retable

E16   Stone carving of the flagellation

Traces of coloured paints remain on the figures.
The underside of the plinth has been burnt in two
places by candles.

PSAS, lx (1925–6), 385–6

E21   Wooden casket

Scotland Early 16th century
64×203×127 mm
Traditionally thought to have belonged to James
IV's Queen, Margaret Tudor, and to have been
given by Queen Mary to the Forresters of
Corstorphine.
The Earl of Verulam (Baron Forrester)

On the top a Gothic R and M, each surmounted by a
coronet, are repeated, intertwined with ribbed
bands and interspersed with four-petalled flowers,
leaves and berries. The same letters run round the
front and sides above repeated flowers and flowers on
hearts, while in the centre of the back panel the

E17   Wooden figure

E19   Oak statue of St Andrew

E18   Carved oak Bishop

E22   The cover of the bute mazer

Scotland 16th century
241 mm
(see entry above for *Bute Mazer* (C31) for details of its ownership)

The cover is formed of a circular plate of natural-coloured bone from the jaw of a whale. The underside is plain whilst the top side has been delicately carved in a five-sectioned pattern consisting of pellet ribbing and floral roundels, overlaid with an interlace type pattern in the shape of a cinquefoil with groups of leaves filling the spaces. The silver knop at the centre is riveted to the cover and passes through a small cinquefoil shaped plate.

PSAS, lxv (1930–1), 217–55

E23   Medical texts

Italy *c*. 1400
415 × 560 mm
Glasgow University Library Hunter 35
The book once belonged to Archbishop Schevez of St Andrews. It contains a treatise on epidemic disease by Raymond Chalin de Vinario and a dictionary on medicine. The first folio has a miniature portrait of the author who is shown seated in an armchair, reading. He is dressed in a blue gown and wears a crimson cap. There are green leaves on his lap and a basket of similar leaves behind him. The manuscript also has several decorated initials.

Young and Aitken, *MSS in the Hunterian Museum*, 36–38

E24   The Herdmanston breviary

England *c*. 1300
310 × 500 mm
ex Chapel of St Clair at Herdmanston, Midlothian.
Edinburgh, National Library, Advocates 18.2.13A

The breviary contains pages of musical notation to which have been added marginal pen drawings of the

initial appears on a heart. On the underside are two panels, one of interlaced six-strand bands (also appearing on the front) and one of an oak branch. The silver bands round the ends and centre, and the lock plate, are covered with leaf scrolls which include leafy letters M and R.

There is a heavily-restored casket in the British Museum which is similar in character. The decoration of both can be compared with that on the lid of the Bute Mazer.

E21   Wooden casket

E22   The cover of the bute mazer

Virgin and Child, churchmen, a knight and scenes from the Passion, in the fourteenth and fifteenth centuries. These drawings are by a Scottish hand.

McRoberts, *Scottish Medieval Liturgical Books*, no 25

E25 Book of hours

Scotland *c*. 1450
150×220 mm
London, Victoria and Albert Museum Reid 54

The Book of Hours is decorated with miniatures framed by borders and initials which imitate northern French work and were probably the work of a Scottish hand. The calendar contains Scottish saints, for example SS Monan and Baldred who are associated with the Firth of Forth, SS Kentigern and Ninian who are connected with the Lothians, and in the Litany, SS Cuthbert and Giles, patrons of Edinburgh.

Ker, *Medieval MSS*, i, 383; McRoberts, *Scottish Medieval Liturgical Books*, no 45

E26 The Culross psalter

Scotland *c*. 1450–1470?
150×240 mm
ex Culross Abbey
Edinburgh, National Library Advocates 18.8.11

The Psalter may have been written and illuminated at the Cistercian Abbey of Culross which is known to have been a centre of book production in the fifteenth century. It has historiated initials, one of which shows David playing the harp, and decorated borders.

PSAS, li (1916–17), 208–12; McRoberts, *Scottish Medieval Liturgical Books*, no 60

E27 Abbot Bothwell's psalter

Scotland *c*. 1445–1470?
150×200 mm
ex Dunfermline Abbey
Boulogne, Bibliothèque Municipale no 92

It has decorated borders and initials. Commissioned for Richard Bothwell, Abbot of Dunfermline, it may have been made at Culross Abbey nearby.

McRoberts, *Scottish Medieval Liturgical Books*, no 59

E28 Book of hours

Scotland Mid 15th century
200×280 mm
Edinburgh, University Library no 42

The book has several full page miniatures, including a miniature of St Ninian, as well as border decorations, all executed in a rough style, characteristic of much Scottish painting of the period.

Borland, *Western Medieval MSS*, 69–73; McRoberts, *Scottish Medieval Liturgical Books*, no 44

E29 Calendar and astronomical tables etc

Scotland Late 15th century (1482?)
180×320 mm
ex Coupar Angus Abbey
Edinburgh, University Library no 126

The manuscript includes painted tables showing the waxing and waning of the moon during the year and also a 'medical' section which has a diagram of a naked man with the main veins drawn in, for use in blood letting. The calendar conforms to the type used by the Cistercians and includes some Scottish entries.

An inscription on folio 1 reads: Liber Beate Marie de Cupro

E28   Book of hours

E30   The Arbuthnott missal

Scotland, Arbuthnott 1491
300×540 mm
ex Arbuthnott Parish Church
Paisley, Museum and Art Galleries

The most handsome of the three manuscripts written by James Sibbald, vicar of St. Ternan's church, Arbuthnott. The Missal has similar border and initial decoration but it is more finely executed than the Psalter and the Hours. The full-page miniature of St Ternan is also more expertly painted. The illuminator of this manuscript may have been a Fleming or else a Scot knowledgeable about Flemish book painting.

PSAS, xxvi (1891–2), 89–90; McRoberts, *Scottish Medieval Liturgical Books*, no 72

E31   The Arbuthnott hours

Scotland, Arbuthnott 1471–84
280×400 mm
ex Arbuthnott Parish Church
Paisley, Museum and Art Galleries

The Book of Hours was probably written by James Sibbald, vicar of the church of St Ternan at Arbuthnott who also wrote the Psalter and Missal of the same name. The Hours has six miniatures including one of St Ternan in a rough style, imitative of Flemish work and likely to be by a Scottish hand. The decorated initials and borders are close to those in the Arbuthnott Psalter. The miniature showing the Mass of St Gregory is the only known picture of a medieval altar painted by a Scottish hand.

PSAS, xxvi (1891–2), 91–92; McRoberts, *Scottish Medieval Liturgical Books*, no 68

E32   The Arbuthnott psalter

Scotland, Arbuthnott 1482
229×292 mm
ex Arbuthnott Parish Church
Paisley, Museum and Art Galleries

Written by James Sibbald, and decorated with border ornament and illuminated initials resembling those in the Arbuthnott Hours.

PSAS, xxvi (1891–2), 90–91; McRoberts, *Scottish Medieval Liturgical Books*, no 69

E30   The Arbuthnott missal

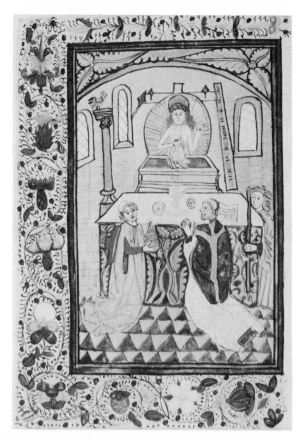

E31 The Arbuthnott hours

E33 James IV's ratification of the marriage contract with Margaret Tudor

Scotland, Stirling? 1502
580×810 mm approx
London, Public Record Office E/39/81

The document was illuminated by sir Thomas Galbraith who was a clerk of the Chapel Royal, Stirling around 1500. The left margin is filled with naturalistic floral decoration composed of intertwining roses and thistles, and a panel with the Arms of Scotland supported by unicorns over a clump of thistles below which are the crowned initials IM for James and Margaret.

Records of payments to the illuminator show that he also decorated a breviary and a gospel book for the king.

E34 Scotichronicon

Scotland 1510
430×700 mm
Edinburgh University Library, no 186

This Scotichronicon was written by Robert Scot and

has two main pages of illustration at the end of the manuscript: a family tree of the Scottish Kings and Queens from Malcolm Canmore and Margaret to James II with roundels enclosing sketchy pen-drawn 'portraits', and a family tree of the Kings of France. Another substantial piece of decoration in the book is the initial on folio 1 which is ornamented with leaves and a face. Elsewhere there are decorative capitals touched with red or blue.

Borland, *Western Medieval MSS*, 272–4

E35 Cartulary of Aberdeen cathedral

Scotland begun *c*. 1544–50
290×400 mm
ex Aberdeen Cathedral
Aberdeen University Library no 248

The Cartulary was begun by Alexander Galloway who was 'rector a Kinkell'. It has illuminated initials with, among other motifs, grotesques, arms, and a small picture of St Michael and the Dragon under a cusped arch.

James, *Medieval MSS*, 76–77

E36 Cartulary of Scone abbey

Scotland 15th–16th century
300×420 mm
ex Scone Abbey
Edinburgh, National library of Scotland Advocates 34.3.28

The manuscript is decorated with some elaborate calligraphic initials with drawings of faces contained in, or attached to, them as well as some marginal pen drawings.

Davis, *Medieval Cartularies*, no 1180

E37 The Scone choirbook

Scotland Early 16th century
390×615 mm
ex Scone Abbey
Edinburgh, National Library of Scotland Advocates 5.1.15

The paper manuscript contains masses and motets written for use at the Chapel Royal at Stirling or else perhaps Scone Abbey. It comprises works of Dufay, Fayrfax and Robert Carver, Canon of Scone Abbey. It is decorated with red initials some of which are embellished with faces.

McRoberts, *Scottish Medieval Liturgical Books*, no 126

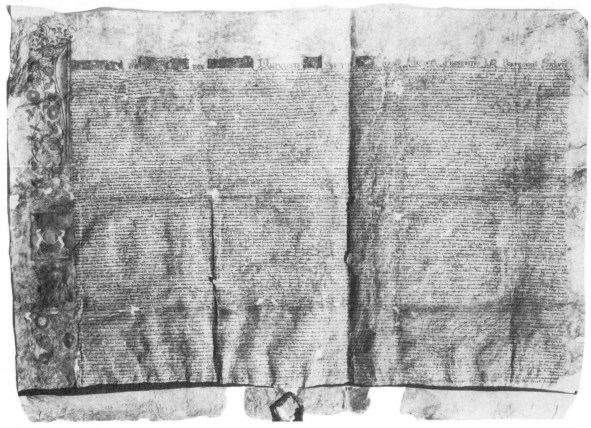

E33　James IV's ratification of the marriage contract with Margaret Tudor

E38　Register of the Chapel Royal, Stirling

Scotland Early 16th century
360×550 mm
ex Stirling, Chapel Royal
Edinburgh, National Library of Scotland Advocate 34.1.5

The Register is decorated with calligraphic initials. The initial shown has leaf-work of a late Gothic type similar to designs found on contemporary wood-work.

Davis, *Medieval Cartularies*, no 1184

E39　The Kinloss or Boswell psalter

Scotland *c*. 1500
300×420 mm
London, Victoria and Albert Museum Reid 52

The psalter is decorated with a miniature of David playing the harp surrounded by a border with

naturalistic floral decoration and also nine pages with large illuminated initials containing flowers. It is probably Scottish work and was made for a Cistercian monastery, probably Kinloss.

McRoberts, *Scottish Medieval Liturgical Books*, no 63; Ker, *Medieval MSS*, i, 383

E40　Andrew Lundy's primer

Scotland *c*. 1500
175×220 mm
Edinburgh, National Library of Scotland Dep 221/5 (B Coll 5)

This book of hours was made for one Andrew Lundy and contains devotions to saints including St Ninian. There is a miniature of St Ninian and others showing the Annunciation, the Virgin and Child, St Jerome and St Anne. The decorated borders of the manuscript comprise naturalistic representations of a variety of flowers including pansies and poppies.

McRoberts, *Scottish Medieval Liturgical Books*, no 49; *Innes Rev*, xi (1960), 39–51; Ker, *Medieval MSS*, ii, 122–4

E39   The Kinloss or Boswell psalter

E41   The Glenorchy psalter

Scotland Later 15th century
241×171 mm
London, British Library, Egerton 2899

The calendar of the psalter contains many Scottish saints, for example SS Fillan, Duthac, Margaret, Serf and Blane. It is decorated with large coloured initials of a crude design and some marginal patterns.

On the fly leaf is a poem associated with St. Columba which is written in Irish (*c.* 1500).

Cat Additions to MSS in BM, 411–13

E42   Scotichronicon

Scotland 15th century
300×410 mm
ex Inchcolm Abbey
Cambridge, Corpus Christi College no 171. By kind permission of the Master and Fellows.

The text of this Scotichronicon, a history of Scotland by John of Fordun, is accompanied with lively, original coloured drawings by a Scottish hand, dating to *c.* 1425. The opened page shows Princess Scota, daughter of the Pharoah of Egypt, landing on the shores of Scotland to which she supposedly gave her name.

Other illustrations in the manuscript include the coronation and funeral procession of Alexander III and the Battle of Bannockburn.

James, *MSS in Corpus Christi College*, 390–5

E43   Scotichronicon

Scotland 1497
ex Inchcolm Abbey
London, British Library Harley 4764

Scotichronicon written by Richard Striveling for George Brown, bishop of Dunkeld (1483–1515). It has decorated initials.

Cat Harleian MSS, iii, 200

E40   Andrew Lundy's primer

E42　Scotichronicon

E44　Lives of the Bishops of Dunkeld

Scotland 16th century
205×320 mm
Edinburgh, National Library of Scotland 34.5.4

The lives of the Bishops of Dunkeld is an account of the administration of the See of Dunkeld during the life of Alexander Mylne, its author and one time clerk to the Bishop of Dunkeld, who died *c*. 1548–49. The accounts seem to have been taken over by an assistant, Thomas Browne, before Mylne's death.

The decoration of the book includes illuminated borders and initials. The frontispiece is painted with two mitred coats of arms of Bishops Gavin Douglas (1515–1522) and George Browne (1483–1515) surmounted by a shield with the arms of Scotland, crowned.

The book once belonged to the Sinclairs of Roslin.

Hannay, *Rentale Dunkeldense*, p xii.

E45　Inventory of cathedral treasury of Aberdeen

Scotland 1549
380×230 mm
Aberdeen University Library no 250

The inventory of the Cathedral treasury was compiled by Alexander Galloway in 1549 and is decorated with coats of arms and illuminated initials. Most of the initials have a blank shield surmounted by a mitre.

James, *Medieval MSS*, 85

E46　Calendar and martyrology

Scotland after 1552?
290×420 mm
ex Elgin Cathedral
Edinburgh University Library no 50

The manuscript was probably written for Elgin Cathedral. It has some rough decoration in a Scottish hand.

PSAS, ii (1854–7), 256–72; Borland, *Western Medieval MSS*, 92–93

E47　Cartulary (*Registrum Capelanorum Chori Ecclesiae Cathedralis Aberdonensis*)

Scotland Late 15th century and later
257×354 mm

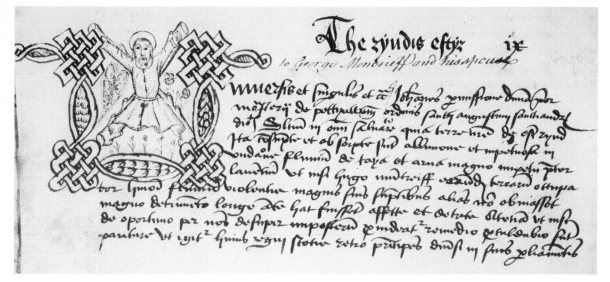

E48   The Pittenweem cartulary

ex Aberdeen Cathedral
Aberdeen University Library no 249

A register of the church choir of Aberdeen Cathedral decorated with painted initials comprising the arms of Bishops of Aberdeen, Elphinstone, Lindesay and Dunbar, dating to the sixteenth century.

James, *Medieval MSS*, 77–85

E48   The Pittenweem cartulary

Scotland 16th century
390×500 mm
St Andrews University Library no 37521

The cartulary has calligraphic decoration around the initials including a large initial with a pen drawing of St Andrew.

E49   Compendium theologice veritatis

Scotland 16th century
290×430 mm
Edinburgh University Library no 72

An inscription on folio 3 of the manuscript tells us that this compendium of theology was once in the hands of Robert Ferguson, prior of Dunfermline (about 1530). The book has a few ornamented initials in its first pages.

Borland, *Western Medieval MSS*, 123

E50   The Orygynale Cronykyl of Scotland

Scotland Later 15th century
280×410 mm
London, British Library Royal 17

A chronicle of Scotland written by Andrew of Wyntoun, canon of St Andrews and prior of St Serf's Inch, Loch Leven, for Sir John Wemyss (died 1428). It is decorated with flowers in a manner resembling the border decoration of the Arbuthnott Hours from Paisley Museum.

Warner and Gilson, *Western MSS*, ii

E51   Psalter and hours

The Low Countries? 15th century
140×250 mm
ex Aberdeen, Hospital of Bishop Dunbar (founded 1531)
Edinburgh, National Library of Scotland Advocates 18.8.14

The psalter has decorated initials and borders with foliage and flower ornament. One of the pages also has a shield with the arms of Scotland in the lower border.

McRoberts, *Scottish Medieval Liturgical Books*, no 40

E52   The Aberdeen hours

The Low Countries Mid 15th century
140×250 mm
London, Victoria and Albert Museum Reid 53

The manuscript, which was probably made in the Netherlands, has decorated borders and initials including an initial with St Nicholas, and also a miniature of the Virgin and Child enthroned. There are Scottish additions dating to pre-Reformation times; a long rubric in the Scots language and an unfinished painting of St Christopher.

Inscriptions show that the manuscript was in the neighbourhood of Aberdeen in the sixteenth and seventeenth centuries.

Ker, *Medieval MSS*, i, 383; McRoberts, *Scottish Medieval Liturgical Books*, no 57

E53 Hours of James IV and Margaret Tudor

Low countries, Ghent/Bruges 1503–1513
200×300 mm
Vienna, Österreichische Nationalbibliothek no 1897

This Book of Hours was made for Margaret Tudor and James IV, for the occasion of their marriage in 1503. It is perhaps the finest medieval manuscript to have been commissioned for Scottish use. Every single page is richly decorated. The borders are painted with naturalistic flowers or leaf patterns, Gothic lettering, geometric designs or representations of jewelry. The paintings surrounding the text show biblical or secular subjects. The calendar for each month contains a miniature of an empty landscape inset with a sign of the zodiac, bordered by monochromatic representations in medallions or niches of events appropriate to the text.

There are nineteen full miniatures in the book, each rendered with a high degree of naturalism and attention to detail. Three of the miniatures in particular are concerned with the king and queen. One of these shows the royal arms of the king (folio 14v) which is framed by a border decorated with the thistle and the marguerite; the monogram IM for James and Margaret, which occurs in other borders in the book, and also in the decoration of the James IV Ratification of the marriage contract, the emblem of St Andrews Cross and the quartered lozenge of the queen's arms. The other two miniatures show James IV and Margaret at prayer. In the miniature of James at prayer (folio 24v) the king is kneeling before an image of Christ as Salvator Mundi to whom he is presented by his patron, St James, dressed as a pilgrim. The miniature of Queen Margaret at prayer (folio 243v) shows the queen kneeling before an apparition of the 'Beata Maria in Sole'. She is attended by a young man in deacon's dress who may be St Cyriac or a guardian angel.

The miniatures of the Royal couple may be compared with the portraits of James III and Margaret of Denmark at prayer in the Trinity College Church Triptych painted by Hugo Van der Goes (1479?) in the National Gallery of Scotland. It is likely that the compositions of the panels, which show the king and queen kneeling before their prie-dieus and attended by their patron saint, influenced these miniatures. This Book of Hours, which Margaret seems to have passed on to her younger sister, Mary Tudor, was illuminated by artists of the Ghent/Bruges school of illumination, possibly Gerard Horenbout and Simon Bening.

Innes Rev, xi (1960), 3–21

E54 Dean Brown's book of hours

The Low Countries? *c.* 1498
125×220 mm
Edinburgh, National Library of Scotland no 10270

The Book of Hours was commissioned for James Brown, Dean of Aberdeen Cathedral, in the last decade of the fifteenth century. The miniature shown here represents his presentation by an episcopal patron saint to the Virgin and Child. The border surrounding the miniature is decorated with a variety of naturalistically painted flowers, which include, for example, a rose, a snowdrop, a hyacinth and a daisy.

The illumination of the manuscript is in the Ghent/Bruges style. It is atelier work and was probably commissioned by Brown during his stay in the Low Countries.

Innes Rev, xix (1968), 144–67

E55 The Perth psalter

The Low Countries? 1450–1500
140×200 mm
ex Perth Parish Church
Edinburgh National Library of Scotland no 652

The Psalter is decorated with illuminated initials and also some borders with vine-leaf decoration. It was evidently made for use in Perth, for the calendar bears a dedication to the parish church there. The style is slightly rough. It may be Scottish work using a Flemish model.

PSAS, lxvi (1931–2), 426–41; McRoberts, *Scottish Medieval Liturgical Books*, no 64.

E56 The Epistolary of Aberdeen cathedral

The Low Countries, Antwerp 1527
390×500 mm
Aberdeen University Library no 22

This epistolary was commissioned in Antwerp by Bishop Gavin Dunbar. It is illuminated with decorated initials and borders and the first page has the arms, motto and initials of Gavin Dunbar surrounded by a border with flowers, a spider and a caterpillar.

E57 Lectures on logic

The Low Countries, Louvain 1477
290×490 mm
Edinburgh University Library no 205

The manuscript was written by a Scot, Magnus Makculloch, in Louvain, and has some rough intitials and headpieces with drawings in black and red ink. The most successful of these is a representation of the Virgin and Child with symbols of the evangelists.

Borland, *Western Medieval MSS*, 291–6

E58 Commentaries on Aristotle's physics

The Low Countries, Louvain *c.* 1467
220×300 mm
ex library of Robert Anderson, a regent of St Salvator's College, St Andrews
Aberdeen University Library no 109

The book was written by George of Moray and contains some poor but interesting drawings, including some of masters and students at work.

Ker, *Medieval MSS*, ii, 2–3

E59 Book of hours

France? 15th century
210×290 mm
London, British Library Add 39761

The manuscript contains devotions suited to Scottish use including a suffrage to Queen Margaret of Scotland and the offices of St George and St Ninian. The miniature of Queen Margaret shows her wearing a cloak with the lion rampant and the tressured border of the arms of Scotland. There are twenty-eight other miniatures, each having wide borders of foliage scrolls, fruit and flowers. All the miniatures are in the French style but are not of very high quality. There are illuminated initials throughout.
 The book was probably made for a Scottish Lady.

Cat Additions to MSS in BM, 179

E60 Virgil

France *c.* 1450–1475?
230×280 mm
Edinburgh University Library no 195

A manuscript of Virgil's works probably written in Paris. It is decorated with three large miniatures, at the beginning of each of the three poems, with naturalistic landscapes and figures. Throughout the manuscript there are decorated and historiated

E59 Book of hours

initials, in a style imitative of William Vrelant, the Flemish artist. The frontispiece to the Aeneid on folio 65 shows the reception of Aeneas by Dido at Carthage. Eight or nine boat loads of soldiers are arriving. Aeneas and Dido meet at the gates of the city. On the right, servants prepare a feast. The book was made for a member of the Scottish Royal family. One page shows the Scottish royal arms. Elsewhere there are the initials PL in a border which perhaps stand for Princess Leonara (or Eleanor), daughter of James I.

Borland, *Western Medieval MSS*, 281–3

E61 The Playfair hours

N France Late 15th century
180×250 mm
London, Victoria and Albert Museum L 475–1918

This Book of Hours and another in Edinburgh University Library (no 43) are very similar in E63 decoration and are likely to have been made in the same workshop, possibly in Rouen, for a Scottish customer. The Playfair Hours has many miniatures and decorated borders, and the calendar is illustrated with scenes of the labours of the months

E60   Virgil

and zodiacal signs. As with the Edinburgh University Library Hours there are entries for several Scottish and English saints.

Ker, *Medieval MSS*, i, 389; McRoberts, *Scottish Medieval Liturgical Books*, no 47

E62   Robert Blackadder's prayerbook

N France 1484–1492
192×290 mm
Edinburgh, National Library of Scotland no 10271

The book was commissioned specially for Robert Blackadder, Bishop of Glasgow. One page shows the owner kneeling before a crucifix in a half-page miniature. The border work comprises large semi-fleur-de-lis motifs amongst scrolls of foliage typical of Northern French work of the later fifteenth century. There are historiated initials containing figures of St Ninian and St Margaret.

E63   Book of hours

N France, Rouen? Late 15th century
210×280 mm
Edinburgh University Library no 43

The Book of Hours was made in France for Scottish use and has Scottish names in the calendar. Like its sister, the Playfair hours, the Edinburgh Hours is full of miniatures and border decorations of a high quality. The illustrations for the labours of the months and zodiacal signs follow the same model as the Playfair hours and are executed in a similar style. This manuscript also once had a miniature of St Ninian with a suffrage to the Saint which has been removed.

The best miniatures include The Shepherds watching their flocks (f 50v), The Annunciation (f 28), St George fighting the dragon (f 144) and a spectacular representation of the 'Beata Maria in Sole', a devotional image of the Virgin with the Child in her arms, standing on a crescent moon and surrounded by rays of light, crowned by two angels (f. 25v).

Borland, *Western Medieval MSS*, 73–78

E61   The Playfair hours

E63   Book of hours

E64   The Talbot hours

N France Mid 15th century
235×240 mm
Edinburgh, National Library of Scotland Dep 221/1
(Blair's College 1)

The decoration of this Book of Hours is of high
quality with finely executed borders, historiated
initials, and miniatures. It was made with a Scottish
owner or owners in mind. The Scottish Royal Arms
have been specially added on one page.

It is closely related to Mss Add. 176 and 177 in the
Fitzwilliam Museum, Cambridge.

Ker, *Medieval MSS*, ii, 113–18

E65   Polychronicon

England Early 15th century
710×410 mm
Aberdeen University Library no 21

The manuscript belonged to John Lord Hay of
Yester in 1554. It is decorated with an historiated
initial, border illumination and an illustration of the
ark. The *Polychronicon* was a widely read history
compiled in the fourteenth century by an
Englishman, Ralph Higden.

James, *Medieval MSS*, 106–8

E66   The Haye manuscript

Scotland *c.* 1480–1495
400×290 mm
Abbotsford Trust (per the National Library of Scotland)
TD 209

A leather binding made by Patrick Lowes enclosing
a translation into Scots of three medieval treatises by
Gilbert Haye. The binding is the earliest Scottish
example to survive and is also unique in being the
only fully signed binding made in Britain before
1500, and the only one of its period in Europe which
is decorated with as many as thirty-three stamps.

The original face of the binding has a central panel
of four horizontal rows of five apostle stamps, eight
of which are repeated. Above are the words Jhesus,
Maria, Johannes, and below: Patricius Lowes me
ligavit. The panel is framed with successive borders
of pattern stamps including animals and foliate
designs. At the head and foot is a row of Tudor roses
and smaller motifs. The whole is framed by double
intersecting fillets with rosettes and Tudor roses at
the corners and scroll stamps with the names Jhesus,
Maria, and Johannes, alternating with a composite
stamp with the monogram IHS.

The tools used on the binding came from Cologne
and the design of the stamps also emanates from
Cologne or Erfurt.

Mitchell, *Scottish Bookbinding*, 1–4, pl 1

E67   Burgh court book of Dunfermline

Europe, or England 1488–1584
400×300 mm
Edinburgh, Scottish Record Office B20/10/11

A bookbinding decorated on one side (upper cover)
with a central panel within a blank frame enclosing
three stamps. These show, at the top, the Virgin and
Child seated between St Barbara and St Catherine,
and at the foot the Adoration of the Magi. The stamp
in the centre shows a domestic interior which is not
thought to have any biblical significance: an old
woman has fallen asleep whilst turning a spit on
which a fowl roasts over the fire. A dog is about to
steal the fowl.

The shape of the stamps on the binding, which are
segments of a circle, may have been designed as
stamps for leather covers for pyramidal boxes such as
church pyxes.

E67   Burgh court book of Dunfermline

The binding may have come from Dunfermline Abbey, but it cannot be considered Scottish. It belongs to a type more usually found on the Continent or in England.

Mitchell, *Scottish Bookbinding*, 7–10, pl 3

E68   Leather seal case

Scotland 15th century
From charter of David of Huntingdon, *c.* 1170.
Edinburgh, National Museum, L.1967

This case was made to protect the seal attached to a 12th-century document. It is globular in shape, in two halves, decorated with cherries.

E69   Three maces of St Andrews university

Scotland and France 15th century
1.282 m, 1.62 m and 1.27 m
St Andrews University

The Mace of the Faculty of Arts, the earliest of the group, was made in France between 1414 and 1418. It is of silver, partially gilt, and has a hexagonal tabernacle type head in three stages. In the lowest stage six demi-angels hold shields, formerly enamelled, which bear the arms of 1) Scotland 2) Bishop Wardlaw (1403–40) 3) Earl of Mar (d 1435)4) Earl of Douglas (d 1424) 5) Duke of Albany (d 1419). Another shield bears the arms and initials of John Spottiswoode, the seventeenth-century Archbishop, and is an addition. The stage above has six figures of saints, two of which (the Virgin Mary and St Michael) are executed in basse taillé enamel and the others (John the Baptist, The Virgin and Child, St Andrew and St Leonard) are executed in champlevé enamel. The final stage is decorated with imitation Gothic traceried windows.

The silver-gilt *Mace of the College of St Salvator* was made, according to the inscription on the foot, by Jean Mayelle, a Parisian goldsmith, in 1461. The stem is decorated with spiral bands of ornament with columbine flowers and repeated letters JK for Bishop Kennedy. The head of the mace is an elaborate hexagonal shrine. On three of the faces are the figures of a bishop, a king and a mendicant friar and the three remaining faces have grotesque figures holding shields with respectively, the arms of Bishop Kennedy, those of St Andrews and the design of an imperial orb within a tressure flory-counter-flory. The last two are later additions. In the central niche is a figure of the Saviour, St Salvator. The knops on the stem of the mace show figures of angels reading and men preaching or reading or lecturing. The medal attached to the stem states that the mace was commissioned by James Kennedy, the founder of the college.

The Mace of the Faculty of Canon Law, which is silver, partially gilt, bears a marked resemblance to the earlier Mace of the Faculty of Arts. The tabernacle-head is similarly divided into three stages with the lowest stage occupied by angels, the second

E69   Three maces of St Andrews university

stage containing figures of saints (St Andrew, St Peter, St Mungo and St John the Baptist), the Madonna and Child, and the Trinity. It is thought that this mace is Scottish workmanship. Since it has no hallmark it was probably made before 1457 when hallmarks were imposed by Act of Parliament. The foot is a later addition. It is less well preserved than the other maces.

PSAS, xxvi (1891–2), 444–74

E70 The mace of Glasgow university
France Mid 15th century
1.447 m
Glasgow University

The mace is similar in design to the Mace of the Faculty of Arts, St Andrews University. It is of silver partially gilt. In the lowest stage of the tabernacle are six angels holding shields bearing the arms of 1) Douglas of Dalkeith, 2) the Regent Morton, 3) James, first Lord Hamilton, 4) The Arms of Scotland, 5) Bishop Turnbull (founder of the University). The last Shield is engraved with the inscription: 'Haec Virga fuit publicis Academiae Glasguensis Sumptibus AD 1465, in Galliam ablata AD 1560; et Academiae restituta AD 1590!' (This mace was made at the public expense of Glasgow University AD 1465, removed to France AD 1560, and restored to the University AD 1590).

The ornamentation of the second stage with engraved panels probably dates to the time of the restitution mentioned in the inscription.

PSAS, xxvi (1891–2), 475–82

E71 The Glenlyon brooch
Scotland *c*. 1500
76 mm
Belonged formerly to the Campbells of Glenlyon.
London, British Museum

A large silver gilt ring brooch with a central cross-bar and two pins. The ring is set with pearls on tall collets, crystals and an amethyst, and the bar has two groups of cloisons, one a replacement, both now lacking their stones. The back of the brooch is chased with nine kidney shaped panels—reminiscent of those on the Kindrochit brooch—containing a black letter inscription with the names of the Magi and the Consumatum—the last saying of Christ.

E72 The Kindrochit brooch
Scotland Late 15th century
88 mm
Found during excavations in the pit prison of

E71   The Glenlyon brooch

Kindrochit Castle, Braemar, Aberdeenshire.
Edinburgh, National Museum NGA 153

A silver-gilt brooch with a scalloped edge and six kidney shaped bezels each set with a flat plate, engraved with an inscription in Gothic ribbon letters and foliaceous designs. The inscription is in blundered French and states: 'I am in place of a friend'.

PSAS, lx (1925–6), 118–22

E73 Silver gilt reliquary cross
Scotland 15th century
42×30×6 mm
From Threave Castle, Kirkcudbrightshire.
Edinburgh, National Museum KE 3

A maltese cross, gilt all over, decorated with quatrefoils and trefoils reserved against a background of cross-hatching. At the top there is a suspension loop for a chain and at the end of each of the remaining three arms are short spikes which were probably meant for securing precious stones or silver balls, as on the comparable Mylecharaine Cross from the Isle of Man (Manx Museum, Douglas). Gems or pearls may also have been attached to the cross at the junctions of the arms. The cross is hollow, and the back is formed of a separate plate. It probably originally contained a relic like a piece of the true cross or the piece of stone from Calvary contained in the similar fifteenth-century reliquary cross from Clare Castle, Suffolk.

Med Archaeol, xxv (1981), 106–07

E72   The Kindrochit brooch

E74   Silver locket

Scotland 15th century
28×17×4.5 mm
From Threave Castle, Galloway.
Edinburgh, National Museum

A rectangular silver locket with a suspension loop. On one side *ihs* in black letter is reserved against a background of cross hatching, the other side is engraved with a quatrefoil leaf design with small trefoils between the leaves. This side slides out. A reliquary or momento would have been kept inside.

Med Archaeol, xxv (1981), 106, fig 9.

E75   Silver-gilt pendant

Scotland 15th century
15 mm
Found in Dundee.
Edinburgh, National Museum KE 5

A small engraved circular pendant with on one side

E75   Silver-gilt pendant

the sacrament monogram 'IHC' and on the other the *Agnus Dei*. It was probably made to contain wax from the Paschal Candle, consecrated at Rome.

E76 Silver rosary crucifix

15th–16th century
58×74 mm
Craigmillar Castle, Edinburgh
Edinburgh, National Museum KE 16

The crucifix has traces of niello inlay and the cross has foliate ends on its arms and base. The upper part is missing. The ebony backing is 19th century. The Christ perhaps copies some noted 12th-century rood and is a memento from a pilgrimage.

E77 Badge of jet

Spain? 15th century
Edinburgh, National Museum KH 5

A small pilgrim's badge—a token for accomplishing the pilgrimage. It is made of jet in the form of a scallop shell and mounted in silver with the letters IHS engraved on the back. The silver mounting is probably Scottish work.

The scallop shell was the sign of St James at Compostella in Spain.

PSAS, xxiv (1889–90), 411

E78 Finger rings

Scotland 14th–16th century
Edinburgh, National Museum NJ 68/124/90/54/7/72/ 61/73

The group of eight rings comprises:

NJ 68
A stirrup shaped gold ring with a square bezel set with a natural octohedral diamond crystal. 14th century. Found in the garden of Holyrood Palace.

NJ 124
A gold ring with a rose-styled bezel engraved in the centre with a cross. The band is engraved with the words AVE M[ARIA] GRAC. 14th century. Found at Weisdale Voe, Shetland.

PSAS, xci (1957–8), 193–4

NJ 90
An iconographical ring of silver gilt, with a centrally-ridged bezel engraved on one side with the Virgin and Child and on the other with the Angel of the Annunciation. 15th century. Found at Hume Castle, Berwickshire.

E76   Silver rosary crucifix

E77   Badge of jet

NJ 61

Betrothal ring with a fede and small nielloed panels around the hoop bearing single letters I I IESUS NA; a shortened form of the talismanic inscription IESUS NAZARENUS REX IUDEOREM often found on medieval brooches is also common on this type of ring. Late 15th century. Provenance unknown.

NJ 73

A gold finger ring with a quatrefoil bezel set with an uncut ruby. 16th century. Found at Dunkeld Cathedral.

PSAS, lx (1925–6), 13

E79   **Bronze cross**

Scotland 15th century
38 mm
From Urquhart Castle, Inverness-shire.
Edinburgh, National Museum HY 12

A pendant bronze cross with a lozenge shaped perforation in the centre. The arms terminate in trefoils with a circular perforation in the middle of each. The attachment for a chain fits through one of these.

E80   **Bone Christ from crucifix**

Scotland 15th century
80 mm
Found at Kirkton of Craig, Montrose, Angus.
Edinburgh, National Museum KE 13

All that remains is the head and torso. Christ is shown with long hair and a beard, and a crown of thorns. His head rests on one shoulder. He is wearing a loin cloth.

E81   **Bronze ewer or laver**

English? 14th century
240 mm
From Bannockburn House, Stirlingshire.
London, British Museum

A bronze tripod laver decorated on the broadest part

NJ 54

An iconographical finger ring with a bezel similar to the above, engraved with the Madonna and Child and an ecclesiastic. The figures are reserved in metal against a black enamel background. The band is ornamented with enamelled stripes. Mid 15th century. Found in the ruins of a cottage at Broughty Ferry [not Melrose, Oman].

PSAS, xix (1884–5), 156–9; Oman, *British Rings*, no 66a

NJ 7

An iconographical ring with a bezel similar to the above engraved on one side with a female figure and on the other, a male figure (Virgin Mary and Angel of the Annunciation?). On the band on each side are engraved enamelled flowers with the initials JR beneath. Mid 15th century. From Tantallon Castle, East Lothian.

PSAS, i (1851–4), 168–9; Oman, *British Rings*, no 66b

NJ 72

A betrothal or love ring with the common fede or hand-in-hand device. The hoop is decorated with a cable pattern on the exterior. Late 15th century. Found in Earnscleuch Water, Lauder.

E80 Bone Christ from crucifix

A hexagonal shaped bronze ewer with a short spout of the zoomorphic type, and a handle. The lid is broken off. There is a very similar ewer, still with its lid, in the Museum Boymans-van Beuminger in Rotterdam.

E83 Bronze ewer

North Europe 15th century
228×130 mm
Found near Traquair, Peeblesshire.
Edinburgh, National Museum KJ 50

An octangular shaped water vessel. The handle and spout are broken off.

E84 Spout of ewer

North Europe 15th century
70 mm
From Bothwell Castle, Lanarkshire.
Edinburgh, National Museum HX 505

The spout resembles the neck and head of a dragon-like animal and is similar to those on medieval bronze ewers, for example on the ewer from Urquhart Castle.

PSAS, xciii (1960–61), pl xvi, fig 1

E81 Bronze ewer or laver

with an inscription in French: IE SUI LAWR IE SERF TUT PAR AMUR CF (I am called a laver, I serve all by love) The spout of the laver is formed of a sinuous neck terminating in a dragon's head, a feature that is often seen in this type of vessel in the fifteenth century. It is held by a short bar fixed to the rim. The handle is decorated on the back with a continuous floral scroll. The lid is missing. Vessels such as these were made in Britain as well as on the Continent, often by the same craftsmen who made bells. The CF in the inscription may be the founder's initials.

Brit Mus Yearbook, ii (1977), 199–201.

E82 Bronze ewer

North Europe 15th century
216×149 mm
From Urquhart Castle, Inverness-shire.
Edinburgh, National Museum HY 5

E82 Bronze ewer

E85 Double spouted ewer

North Europe 15th century
297 mm
Found c. 1840 at Ashkirk, near Selkirk, on the supposed site of a residence of the medieval Bishops of Glasgow.
Private collection (the late Dr Douglas E Ross)

The ewer is made of bronze, stands on three feet

E85   Double spouted ewer

shaped like lion's paws and has a hinged lid. The double animal-headed spout is a remarkable feature as are the angular protuberances that rise from the widest part of each of the six sides. The ewer is a particularly elaborate instance of the medieval tripod ewer.

There is a representation of an identical ewer with a crouching lion on top of its lid in a painting of *c*. 1440 of the Annunciation by the Dutch painter Roger van der Weyden, now in the Louvre, Paris.

PSAS, lxxxiii (1947–8), 240

E86   Bronze aquamanile

North Europe 14th century
215 mm×203 mm
Found in a dug-out canoe in Kilbirnie Loch with a bronze 3-legged pot next to the site of a crannog or lake dwelling.
Edinburgh, National Museum MC 41

The aquamanile is shaped like a lion with a hole in the top of the head once covered by a hinged lid, where the water was put in, and a long spout emanating from the mouth, for pouring. The handle is formed of the lion's tail raised to the head.

PSAS, xiii (1878–9), 54–56

E87   Bronze jug

North Europe Late 15th century
230 mm
Found in Edinburgh when digging foundations of the South Bridge.
Edinburgh, National Museum MC 26

Bronze spouted jug for washing the hands.

E88   Bronze candlestick

North Europe Early 16th century
230 mm
From St Magnus Cathedral, Kirkwall, Orkney.
Edinburgh, National Museum MG 18

Pottery from Bothwell Castle

Scotland 14th–15th century
Edinburgh, National Museum

These pieces of earthenware were recovered along with many more from Bothwell Castle in Lanarkshire, which was, in the 15th century, one of the main Douglas strongholds. It is likely that most of the pottery was manufactured locally and there are indeed documentary references to a potter of Bothwell in the opening years of the 16th century. The form of these pots might suggest a comparison

E86   Bronze aquamanile

with 13th-century English pottery but it is likely
these types remained in use in Scotland much later.

PSAS, lxxxvi (1951–2), 140–70

E89   Earthenware jug

Scotland 14th–15th century
229×286 mm
MEC 55

Wide-bodied, green-glazed jug with face mask at
spout.

E90   Baluster Jug

Scotland 14th–15th century
35 mm
MEC 37

Baluster shaped jug of earthenware with orange and

E87   Bronze jug

E88 Bronze candlestick

green glaze and decorated with incised fern designs. Jugs like this would have been used for drinking.

E91 Earthenware jug

Scotland 14th–15th century
35 mm
MEC 39

Slender pitcher with dark brown-green glaze decorated with strips and impressed circles.

E92 Earthenware jug

Scotland 15th century
280 mm
MEC 145

Jug with brown-green glaze and parrot-beak bridge-spout. It is decorated with three oval finger-impressed pendants.

E93 Earthenware jug

Scotland 14th–15th century
407×350 mm
From Lochleven, Kinross-shire.
Edinburgh, National Museum L.1925.5

Large earthenware pitcher with three handles and a small bridge spout. It is covered in green glaze and decorated with appled strips and pads of a darker clay, forming foliage patterns.

E94 Clay plaque with virgin and child

Germany, the Low Countries or Burgundy? 15th century
154 mm
From the site of the chapel of St Mary, Markle, East Lothian.
Edinburgh, National Museum

The plaque is a matrix for making impressions. It depicts the Virgin and Child seated in a garden, the design of which is closely based on a mid-fifteenth-century engraving by the South German print-maker, the Master ES. Round it is an inscription in French in Lombardie capitals: MON ★ C(U)ER ★ AVERDMON ★ CUER ★ AVE ★ GARDE . . . ★ (My heart, Hail to the Queen of My Heart, Hail Guard . . .)

The Markle plaque was used to make devotional plaques, possibly of papier maché. The use of the plaque at Markle remains a mystery, unless it was to provide pilgrimage souvenirs, if not for Markle itself, for a nearby pilgrimage centre such as Whitekirk.

Pantheon (June 1982)

E95 Seal matrix of Joan Beaufort, queen of James I

Scotland *c.* 1425
19.5 mm
Found at Kinross.
Edinburgh, National Museum NM 163

A gold signet, circular, with two hinged flaps on its back for grasping when in use. The design consists of the impaled arms of Scotland and France and England quarterly surrounded by foliage.

Stevenson & Wood, *Scottish Heraldic Seals*, i, 37

E96 Seal matrix of the chapter of Dunkeld

Scotland 16th century
53 mm
Edinburgh, National Museum NM 17

A brass, circular matrix with a pierced knob on the

E89, E91, E92   Earthenware jugs

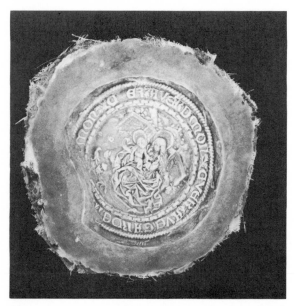

E94   Clay plaque with virgin and child   E94   Clay plaque with virgin and child

back. St Columba is shown as a bishop, with mitre and nimbus, seated on a throne, his right hand raised in benediction, his left holding a crozier. At each side is a half-length figure of an angel waving a thurible, and the words S'COLVMBA.

This the second seal of the chapter of Dunkeld.

Legend: S' CAPITVLI DVNKELD' AD CAVSAS ET CETA NEGOCIA.

Stevenson & Wood, *Scottish Heraldic Seals*, i, 145

E97   Seal matrix of the abbey of Kelso

Scotland 16th century
60 mm (76 mm including pierced lugs)
Edinburgh, National Museum NM 16

A circular brass matrix with four pierced lugs. Within a canopied porch stands the Virgin, with rayed nimbus, holding the Child, also with nimbus, on her left arm. The background is diapered with stars and there are initials at the sides—the letter G reversed, which may refer to the Cardinal de Guise, nominated Commendator of Kelso after 1542. This is the fourth seal of the Abbey.

Legend: S'GILLVM. CONMVNE. STE. MARIE. DE. KELCO.

Stevenson & Wood, *Scottish Heraldic Seals*, i, 188

E98   Seal matrix of the Cistercian abbey of Coupar Angus

Scotland 16th century
59×42 mm
Edinburgh, National Museum NM 160

A silver, vesica-shaped matrix. Within a Gothic niche a figure of the Blessed Virgin seated, holding in her right hand a branch of lilies, and with her left supporting the Infant Jesus standing on the bench beside her; beneath, under an arched niche, the kneeling figure of an Abbot, frontwise, in the attitude of prayer, holding a crozier against his breast. On either side of the recess is an armorial shield; dexter, the arms of Scotland: sinister, three escutcheons (Hay). Beaded borders.

Legend: S' COMVNE: CAP'LI. MON. DE. CVPRO.

Stevenson & Wood, *Scottish Heraldic Seals*, i, 175

E99   Seal matrix of the office of the Prior of Friars preachers of Perth

Scotland 15th century
49×34 mm
Edinburgh, National Museum NM 47

A brass vesica-shaped matrix, with a fixed handle on the back. Within a canopied niche, with tabernacle work at the sides, is a crowned figure of the Virgin holding the Child on her left arm. Beneath, in an arched niche, is a friar kneeling to dexter, looking up in adoration. There is a cabled border within which is the inscription.

Legend: S' OFFICII: PORIS: ORD: PDICARV: DE. PRH

Stevenson & Wood, *Scottish Heraldic Seals*, i, 207

E100   Seal matrix of Burgh of Aberdeen

Scotland 1430
71 mm
Edinburgh, National Museum NM 23, 24
(electrotypes)

Two circular brass matrices, each with four pierced lugs. The obverse shows a shield bearing arms: A castle, triple towered, embattled and masoned, within a royal tressure. Supporters: two lions holding in their mouths, above the shield, an escroll inscribed with the motto, BON ACCORD.

Legend: SIGILLUM COMUNE DE ABERDEN

Reverse: With a niche, showing the front gate and walls of a castle with triple canopy above, is a representation of the miracle of St Nicolas restoring three youths to life. The saint stands in the centre in episcopal vestments, with mitre and nimbus, right hand raised, left holding crozier, on dexter a tub in which stand the 3 youths, foliage and flowers in the background.

Legend: SIGILLUM COMUNE DE ABERDEN

There is an inscription in 2 concentric circles on the back of each matrix: 'the zer of grac M CCCCXXX ion the vanus was alderman and thes selmad'. This is the second seal of the burgh of Aberdeen.

Stevenson & Wood, *Scottish Heraldic Seals*, i, 52

E101   Seal matrix of the Burgh of Crail

Scotland 15th century
68 mm
Edinburgh, National Museum NM 150

The obverse of the seal matrix has a lymphad on the sea with slightly raised prow and stern, mast with sail furled, cordage, and flag bearing a saltire. Above the yard a crescent and eight stars.

Legend: SIGILLVM COMMVNE BVRGI DE KARALE.

Reverse: The Virgin, with crown and nimbus, holding the Child on her left knee, sits on a throne with ornamented back. At each side is an angel swinging a thurible. Beaded borders.

Legend: SIGILLVM COMMVNE BVRGI DE KARALE. This is the second seal of Crail.

Stevenson and Wood, *Scottish Heraldic Seals*, i, 56

E102 Seal matrix of the incorporation of Hammermen of Dundee

Scotland 16th century
39 mm
Edinburgh, National Museum NM 41

A circular brass matrix. Within a canopied niche stands a figure of St Eloi as a bishop, with mitre, holding in his right hand a hammer erect, and in his left a crozier obliquely in front of him. Beneath is a shield bearing arms: A hammer crowned. At each side is a vase of flowers (symbolic of Dundee).

Legend: s' COMUNE ARTIS MALLIATORIUM SCI ELEGI DE DUDE

Stevenson & Wood, *Scottish Heraldic Seals*, i, 60

E103 Coins, David II—James IV

Edinburgh, National Museum

In 1357 denominations greater than a penny were introduced for the first time—groats, half-groats and gold nobles—to correspond with developments in England. The names of some of the late fourteenth-century moneyers are known and in some cases their work can be identified. James Mulekyn of Florence may have been responsible for the new designs of 1357 and his initial I appears on some of the halfpence. His brother Donatus, who probably designed David II's great seal, has left his initial on many of the reverses of this coinage while a B, for Bonagius of Florence who had formerly worked in

the English mint at Florence, appears on some of the coins of Robert II.

Of more interest from a design point of view are the gold lions of Robert III issued from the last years of the fourteenth century. They bear a representation of the crucifixion of St Andrew, a design previously found on the great seal of the realm used in the interregnum after the death of Alexander III.

A high point was reached with the coinage of James III (1460–88). Now for the first time 'true' portraits appear on the thistle groats issued about the 1470s and the type VI groats of the end of the reign. The former may have been the work of Thomas Tod. The bust on the type VI groats is particularly fine and corresponds closely with the portrait of James on the Trinity College Altarpiece.

Two new designs for the gold coins are also of considerable merit. The riders have a spirited representation of the king in armour galloping on horseback while the unicorns have a unicorn holding the royal arms on the obverse and a wavy star on the reverse.

The portraits on James IV's coins return to the conventional full face medieval image but a gold lion was reissued with a new design of St Andrew carrying his cross. To the very end of his reign belongs the pattern for a gold coin that was never issued. It corresponds in type to the contemporary English rose noble and has a depiction of St Michael slaying the dragon on the obverse and a large ship on the reverse—perhaps a representation of the *Michael*, the largest ship in James' fleet.

E104   Medal of Archbishop Schevez of St Andrews

E104   Medal of Archbishop Schevez of St Andrews

E105   Gold medal of the Duke of Albany

E105   Gold medal of the Duke of Albany

E104 **Medal of Archbishop Schevez of St Andrews**

Low Countries 1491
London, British Museum

A rare medal showing the bust of the archbishop in a plain cap and mantle with the legend WILHELMUS + SCHEVEZ + SCI + ADREE + ARCHIEPS and on the reverse his coat of arms on a shield behind which is an archiepiscopal cross and the legend LEGATUS * NATUS * & * TOTIUS REGNI * SCOTIE * PRIMAS * 1491 (Legate by nature (of his office) and Primate of the whole Kingdom of Scotland).

William Schevez was made Archbishop of the see of St Andrews in 1478. He was employed by James IV to aid in negotiations at home and abroad.

The style of the medal compares with some Flemish examples of the period ascribed to Quintin Metsys who worked in Louvain and Antwerp. Schevez was educated in Louvain and when he was summoned to Rome by the Pope in January 1491 he stopped there on his way. It is possible that his own medal was struck by Metsys.

Hawkins, *Medallic Illustrations*

E105 *Gold medal of the Duke of Albany*

France 1524
Edinburgh, National Museum

The medal is one of three known specimens and is thought to have been struck from Scottish gold from

101

Crawford Moor. The obverse shows a shield crowned upon a cross, bearing the arms of John, Duke of Albany impaled with those of Anne, an heiress of John de la Tour, Count d'Auvergne, whom he married in 1505. The legend reads IOANNIS ALBANIE DUC, GUBERN (John Duke of Albany Regent) on the reverse is the Holy Dove with a cross above; below the arms of the Duke within the Order of St Michael, 1524. The legend reads SUB UMBRA TUARUM (Under the shadow of thy [wings])

The medal was struck in the year when the regent returned to France having found the Scottish nobles impossible to govern. The grandson of James II of Scotland, the Duke had been appointed Regent after the death of James IV. He died in Auvergne in 1536.

Hawkins, *Medallic Illustrations*

6 THE MEDIEVAL CHURCH

In the Middle Ages the finest achievements of many artists and craftsmen were much more likely to beautify a church rather than a palace or a house. The Church itself was an important patron of arts and crafts but in addition to that much of the patronage exercised by the laity was not ostensibly for its own benefit but primarily for the honour and glory of God. This often took the form of endowing new churches or beautifying existing ones.

Gold rider of James III, minted *c* 1480

The pre-Reformation church in Scotland, as elsewhere, was the setting for an elaborate liturgy and its interiors were a reflection of the complex religious needs of the communities. The quantity and quality of church furnishings varied enormously but even the humblest of parish churches might have richly painted and carved surfaces, stained glass windows, embroidered hangings and precious communion vessels.

Decoration in the nave was dominated by a profusion of images—mural paintings to instruct the worshippers with stories from the Scriptures or episodes from the lives of the saints, and painted and carved statues of saints and evangelists presided over altars dedicated to them, sometimes by merchant or craft guilds in the burghs, or confraternities (religious societies). They were particularly popular from the fifteenth century onwards as Scotland became influenced by the devotional cults current in Northern European countries such as the Blessed Virgin, Our Lady of Loreto, St Salvator and the Holy Blood.

The nave also contained a font for baptisms and a pulpit in front of the screen. Effigies and monuments to the dead were erected by those who could afford it, mostly the nobles, and placed round the walls or in aisles or transepts off the nave.

The sanctuary of the medieval church, as the exclusive domain of the clergy, received special treatment. It was separated from the nave by the choir or rood screen and a curtain. The screen, made of stone or more usually of wood, was ornately carved and painted. Some rood screens in the larger churches had galleries reached by a narrow stair and accommodated the 'rood altar' and sometimes an organ. A rood or cross, flanked by the figures of St Mary and St John, surmounted the whole. During the mass the laity had a distant and sometimes obscure view of the proceedings in the sanctuary and the door of the screen was kept firmly locked and the curtain drawn when mass was not being celebrated.

In the churches of monks or canons and the new collegiate churches, often endowed by noble families for their souls and the souls of their ancestors, stalls were placed behind the choir screen on the north and south sides of the chancel. Here the canons or monks assembled at set hours of the day and night to recite the Divine Office, composed of psalms, hymns, prayers and scripture readings.

In the fifteenth and sixteenth century the music and ceremonial became more elaborate and so more magnificent surroundings were required, particularly stalls. Those commissioned at this time were often richly carved. The back and end panels and misericords (folding seats) had biblical subjects,

103

104   Choir stalls for the cathedral dignitaries, Dunblane, late 15th century

grotesque figures and foliaceous ornament. The upper parts were made with ornate canopies and crocketed pinnacles.

Near the stalls stood the lectern or reading desk from which the gospel was read. Many of the finer ones, like the one which survives from Holyrood Abbey, were of brass in the form of a spread-winged eagle on top of a pillar.

At the east end of the sanctuary was the high altar usually flanked by the principal image—a painting or sculpture of the patron of the church. The altar was an oblong structure of wood or stone, into the surface of which was set a stone slab incised with crosses. The front was draped with a piece of embroidery or tapestry patterned with some sacred device or even the royal arms. For the mass a large silver or gold cross and two candlesticks, as well as other ornaments and a decorated textus or gospel book, were placed upon the altar. The chalices and patens were normally of silver. There were also sacring bells, ciboria for housing the Host and censers for burning incense. The altar was usually screened off between ceremonies by a curtain, in some of the wealthier churches like St Giles in Edinburgh, supported on brass columns.

The altarpiece placed behind the altar was the pride of the whole church. It was usually the gift of a rich patron and consisted of one or more panels painted with images such as the Madonna and Child, the Saviour of the World and the Holy Trinity. Sometimes the centre piece was of carved wood with painted wings. Another common type of altarpiece was the retable made up of carved stone or wooden panels which narrated the lives of the saints, the Life of Christ or the Passion.

F1   Font

Scotland, West Highland 15th century
0.33 m × 0.47 m
From the churchyard of St Maelrubha, Borline, Skye, Inner Hebrides.
Edinburgh, National Museum KG 1

The font, which stands on a modern pedestal, is carved from stone quarried in the Isle of Harris, Outer Hebrides, and has figure subjects and other designs in high relief on its exterior. These include representations of, the Crucifixion, St Michael slaying the dragon, The Virgin and Child and a mitred bishop (St Maelrubha?). Two panels either side of the Crucifixion are carved with interlace

F1   Font

work. The two other intermediary panels bear worn inscriptions: ioha(nne)s [mac]/clouaud de/ . . . [anno domini] mcc[c]ccx[xx] (Iohannes Macleod of . . . in the year of our Lord 1530)

This John Macleod is probably the John MacLeod of Minginish who seems to have been chief of his clan from about 1552–1557.

On the receding underside of the font, between the figures, are foliaceous designs and a conventional rose. The font was probably originally supported by a base of four columns for which four circular moulded beads remain beneath.

Steer and Bannerman, *Medieval Sculpture in the West Highlands*, no 5

F2   Portable altar

Scotland 13th century
279 × 254 × 38 mm
From Coldingham Priory, Berwickshire.
Edinburgh, National Museum KG 78

The altar is of sandstone, rectangular in shape, with five consecration crosses carved in its top surface— four crosses pattee at the corners with a cross crosslet in the centre. Such altars may have been for carrying from place to place, for use at masses where there was no fixed altar, or else set in timber-topped altars, perhaps sealing consecrated relics.

PSAS, xiii (1879–9), 126

F3   Floor tiles

Scotland 13th century
Found detached, during excavations carried out in 1878 and 1895 at Newbattle Abbey, Midlothian.
Scottish Development Department

A large number of the tiles from the Abbey are mosaic tiles of various shapes originally intended to be placed together in groups ranging from one tile to eight tiles to form continuous geometric patterns. A single large 'wheel' motif, covering one area of floor was composed of seventeen different shapes of tiles set within a circle 1.83 m in diameter.

A number of inlaid tiles were also found, including several small lozenge-shaped tiles inlaid with a rosette ornament, which were incorporated into the wheel pattern. The largest of the inlaid tiles is a rectangular tile with a fleur-de-lis and ring pattern, several of which, when placed together, created a continuous decoration. The inlaying of a pattern in a tile was made by impressing the pattern into the clay, and filling the impression with a different coloured clay, in this case white.

Reconstructions of the patterns composed by the arrangement of tiles found at Newbattle show that a number of them closely resembled patterns in the floor mosaics in the south transept chapels at Byland Abbey, Yorkshire.

PSAS, lxiii (1928–9), 287–92

F4 Floor tiles

Scotland 13th century
Found in the chapter house and in the outer cloister court of Melrose Abbey in the Borders in 1921.
Scottish Development Department

The selection comprises a number of tiles found detached or in fragmentary settings in the Abbey, including mosaic, inlaid and painted tiles which may have been made locally. The mosaic tiles were used in combinations of different shaped tiles to form various continuous geometric patterns and also a single wheel pattern which resembled the one at Newbattle Abbey. Several inlaid tiles were incorporated into some of these patterns, while other decorative schemes were composed solely of inlaid tiles of uniform sizes and designs.

One of the mosaic tile settings from the chapter house consists of a polygonal pattern formed of tiles shaped as triangles, rectangles and inlaid hexagons. It is similar to patterns of tiling at Rievaulx Abbey, Yorkshire, and Newbattle Abbey, Midlothian. A group of painted tiles was also found.

PSAS, lxiii (1928–9), 293–7

F5 Floor tiles

Scotland, North Berwick 13th century
Uncovered in the grounds of a Cistercian Convent in North Berwick.
Edinburgh, National Museum

A selection of tiles including square and oblong border ones which were made in a kiln situated near the north wall of the convent. The relief patterns on the tiles, which project 6 mm above the surface, were made with a wooden stamp or mould. The square tiles have geometric or zoomorphic designs and are of three basic varieties. Several of them are stamped with a pattern composed of interlaced segments which, when placed together, make a continuous decoration of intersecting rings. Another group has a pattern composed of four fleur-de-lis set diagonally on the tile and others are stamped with 'lions' or 'panthers' passants encircled by a foliaceous spray.

The tiles are unusual in Medieval Britain but bear a resemblance to stamped tiles produced in the Rhineland, where it is thought that the stamping method of decorating tiles originated in the twelfth century.

PSAS, lxiii (1928–9), 297–304

F6 Two oak choir stalls

Scotland *c.* 1470
Misericords 0.66×0.28 m
Transferred *c.* 1585 from Lincluden Collegiate Church, Kirkcudbrightshire, to the choir of Terregles Parish Church nearby, where they were preserved until recently.
Edinburgh, National Museum

The Stalls stand on a modern base and are surmounted at the top by a modern rail in place of the original canopies. The handrests and misericords in the lower part are in a good state of preservation. The misericords are carved with a serpent with webbed claws and with a lion-like creature with only two hind legs, respectively.

The framework of the upper part of the stalls is formed of three buttress pilasters decorated with crockets and finials. The outer pilasters have two miniature carved canopies. The middle pilaster has a more ornate canopy, below which the wood is cut away to form a niche for a statuette.

When the stalls were restored in 1875 it was found that two oak planks which formed part of a panel inserted between the pilasters, showed a faint depiction in paint of a crowned female figure with long plaited hair wearing a gown and a mantle fastened at the throat by a brooch. A reconstruction of the painting, which is still incorporated in the stalls, is shown at the side.

PSAS, lxxxii (1947–8), 288–9

F7 Panel with the Arma Christi

Scotland Early 16th century
Formerly in Kirkwall Cathedral, Orkney.
Edinburgh, National Museum KL 19

Part of an oak panel carved with the 'Arma Christi', the five wounds of Christ shown with emblems of The Passion. The hands and feet are pierced; the heart at the centre is surrounded by the crown of thorns and the nails and the dice are carved at the side. The missing part of the panel would have shown the other pierced hand and foot as well as other emblems of the Passion. Representations of the 'Arma Christi', which was a popular devotional image in Northern Europe before the Reformation, are found elsewhere in Scottish art, for example in manuscripts, stone carving and panel painting.

This panel may have formed a bench end in the Cathedral.

PSAS, xc (1956–7), 120

F8 Two carved oak panels

Scotland Early 16th century
0.685×0.457 m
From Seton Collegiate Church, East Lothian.
Edinburgh, National Museum KL 148

Both panels are carved with two ribs set back to back with ornaments in the spaces including leaves, flowers and thistles. One has the 'Arma Christi' over a pierced heart within a crown of thorns and on a

F6   Two oak choir stalls

F7   Panel with the Arma Christi

The door is divided into two rows of three narrow panels and one row of two wide panels. The carving of the framework is similar to the wall-panelling, its distinctive feature being the four-niched interspaces of the six panels, which are unique in Scottish carved doors.

PSAS, xvi (1881–2), 61–8; lxxiii (1938–9), 324–5

F10   The Beaton panels

Scotland or the Low Countries *c.* 1530
Thought to have been taken from Arbroath Abbey to Balfour House, Fife.
Recently moved to Newton Don, Nenthorn, Berwickshire.
Trustees of late Major C J Balfour & Hon Mrs A Balfour

The eight panels originally formed part of a larger section of panelling which has been cut down. The first three are carved respectively with representations of The Annunciation; The Tree of Jesse with Christ at the top in the arms of the Virgin represented as the 'Beata Maria in Sole'; and The Arms of Christ on a Shield supported by angels, below which is a reed, and above, as a crest, other

central shield a griffin (for Lauder?). The other has pierced tracery.

PSAS, xc (1956–7), 121

F9   The Montrose panels and doors

Scotland *c.* 1515
1.384×3.213 m
Found in an old house in Montrose where they had been used as a partition between two garrets. The panels may have come from the hall of a hospital founded by Abbot Patrick Panter of Montrose who was Abbot of Cambuskenneth in 1516.
Edinburgh, National Museum KL 125

The pieces consist of a long section of wall-panelling and a door, both made of oak. The former is carved into eighteen panels set in two rows within a framework. Each section is carved in low relief with a reticulated pattern of thistles, roses, campanulas, vines with grapes and oak sprays pecked by birds and nibbled by swine. A pair of foxes dressed satirically as friars can be seen in two of the panels. One of these groups shows the beasts walking in procession each with a staff. The other shows them holding up a goose between them and their staves, which are crossed saltire-wise. Another panel has the arms of Panter.

108

F8   Two carved oak panels

F9 The Montrose panels and doors

F11 Six carved oak panels

Scotland 16th century
0.628×0.292 m; 0.527×0.292m; 0.52×0.292 m
0.622×0.177 m; 0.495×0.215 m; 0.444×0.292 m
Provenance unknown
Edinburgh, National Museum KL 117–122

Three of the panels are carved with thistle, rose and cone-like designs respectively. Two, which are damaged, have the linen fold design, and one shows a man with a bow and arrow aiming at a bird sitting on a branch of a tree.

PSAS, lxxi (1936–7), 16

F12 Oak panel from Balmerino

Scotland
0.584×0.254 m
Said to have been taken from the parish church in Balmerino, Fife when it was demolished in 1811. It is supposed to have come originally either from Balmerino Abbey or its chapel of St Ayle.
Edinburgh, National Museum KL 90

The panel is carved with various grotesque figures and a female figure grasping what seems to be the tail of a serpent and brandishing a club. In the upper part is a figure of a horseman.

PSAS, xl (1905–6), 12

symbols of the passion and the crown of thorns as a wreath.

Of the remaining panels two are heraldic. One has three shields within fruited branches, the upper shield showing the arms of Beaton over an abbot's crozier flanked by D.B. for David Beaton (Archbishop of St Andrews 1539–46). The other two shields show the arms of his parents.

The next panel shows the royal arms with large unicorn supporters, crowned helm and crest with thistles below and foliate at the sides.

The other panels have scrolls of fruits with thistles and a rose for James V and Margaret Tudor. The last panel has roof bosses mounted on it, showing the Royal Arms, four Beaton shields, *ihs* and *Ma*.

The panels are surrounded by vine sprays. Below them are the upper parts of five panels of elaborate openwork tracery. The style suggests Flemish workmanship.

F10 The Beaton panels

F10   The Beaton panels

F13   Four carved oak panels

Scotland Mid 16th century
0.56×0.75 m, except panel with royal arms; which is
0.8×0.76 m.
From the chapel in the Nunnery, Overgate,
Dundee.
Edinburgh, National Museum

The panels are in a good state of preservation and the
carving, which is in high relief, conveys much fine
detail. The subjects of three of the panels are
biblical. They are: The Judgement of Solomon, The
Annunciation, The Adoration of the Magi.

These panels are medieval in manner but have
some renaissance detail. The costumes reflect
sixteenth-century dress.

The fourth panel is carved with the Royal Arms of
James V supported on either side by unicorns. Below
are four thistles and above is a crowned helm
ornamented with fleur-de-lis and crested with a Lion
Sejant affronté, itself crowned, holding a sceptre and
originally a sword, which is broken off. The

inscription at the top of the panel has been repaired,
and reads IN DEFENS.

PSAS, xx (1885–6), 108–120

F14   Woodwork from St Nicholas' church, Aberdeen

Scotland or Flanders First decade 16th century
From the late medieval choir of St Nicholas Church,
Aberdeen.
Edinburgh, National Museum, KL 105–108

The woodwork comprises:
A remnant of an oak canopy with Gothic pierced
fenestration which originally surmounted a range of
choir stalls (3.25 m long).

Five stiles in the form of spired pinnacles with
gablets and crockets varying in length from 1.295 m
to 1.32 m, which probably formed part of the rood
loft screen and chancel door. A length of foliated and
cusped cresting of about 1.32 m long.

Two lengths (both approx 2.438×0.158 m) of a
rail bearing an inscription in raised Gothic letters.
These formed part of an inscription which ran along
above the eaves of the north side of the choir of St
Nicholas.

F13   Four carved oak panels

F13 Four carved oak panels

The complete furnishing of the choir with the woodwork of the stalls, the screen and the chancel door and other wood parts was the responsibility of John Fendour who was contracted with the Burgh of Aberdeen to do the work on the 26th December 1507. It is thought that the stalls with the canopy fronts were made in Flanders and fitted up by Fendour who probably added some parts which do not reach the high standard of the canopies. Fendour may have come from the Continent. He also did some work for St Machars Cathedral.

PSAS, lxviii (1933–4), 355–66

F15　**Four panels from Dumfriesshire**

Scotland Early 16th century
0.43×0.215　m　(2　panels),　0.508×0.215　m, 0.558×0.222 m
From a stall framework, Dumfries-shire.
Edinburgh, National Museum

The oak panels are all carved with fenestrations of a similar kind. One contains a human heart over two arrows placed Saltire-wise. Two have the sacred monograms *Ihs* and *Ma* respectively and the last has a lozenge with four quatrefoil compartments. This panel, which has recently been cut down in size, is of better quality than the other three.

PSAS, lx (1925–6), 390, fig 4

F13   Four carved oak panels

F16   Three oak misericords

Scotland Late 15th century–Early 16th century
Said to have come from the north east of Scotland.
Kept in Gordon Castle for a number of years.
Edinburgh, National Museum KL 128–30

The brackets of the misericords are each carved with a curved stem terminating at both ends in a spray of leaves. The spray encloses in one, two half human, half animal figures standing on their hind legs grasping a pruned stem or stalk, in the second a dragon-like creature which tramples another, and in the third a demi-angel with wings spread holding a shield parted per pale.

PSAS, lxxiv (1939–40), 151, pl LIX

F17   Oak misericord

Scotland Late 15th century
0.215×0.304×0.05 m
From a choir stall from the South of Scotland.
Edinburgh National Museum

The misericord is carved with a representation of the Adoration of the Magi at the centre of which is the Virgin seated with the Infant on her lap. The head of an ass is behind her to the left and the head of an ox is to the right. One of the kings kneels before the

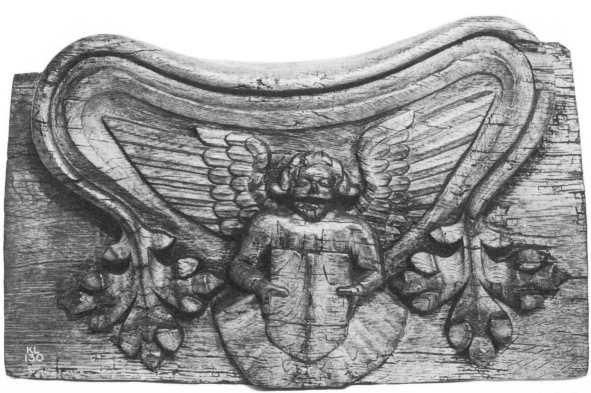

F16   Three oak misericords

F16   Three oak misericords

F16   Three oak misericords

Virgin with a cup from which he removes the lid with the assistance of the Child.

The principle figures are supported by a moulded base. They would have been accompanied by representations of St Joseph and the third king on either side of the bracket.

PSAS, lx (1925–6), 386–8

F18   Two oak misericords

Scotland or England 14th century
Provenance unknown
Edinburgh, National Museum L 1933. 2153–4

One misericord is carved with two branches of acanthus leaf leading from the corners of the bracket

F18   Two oak misericords

F21   Bell

Scotland *c.* 1495
Formerly the bell of Dundonald Parish Church, Ayrshire where it was used until 1841. Transferred to Dundonald Free Kirk after 1843 where it hung for forty years.
Edinburgh, National Museum (1967)

The bell is of cast bronze with an out-turned sound bow. Beneath a band of moulded decoration on the

and meeting at the centre. The supporter on the right of the bracket is a woman's head in a wimple. The left support is broken off.

The other misericord is carved with a beast with arms instead of forelegs; the right arm stretches along its back to grasp the tail. The feet are human; the head, mitred. It is supported on the left by a mitred face with long hair. The right hand supporter is missing.

The misericords closely resemble some of a similar date in Chichester Cathedral, Sussex.

F19   Five fragments of wooden altar retables

Scotland and the Low Countries Early 16th century
KL 7 from the Bell Collection. Provenance of others unknown.
Edinburgh, National Museum KL 7, 8, 12, 13

Four of the fragments in the group, showing part of an 'Entombment' (365×125 mm), part of a 'Descent into limbo' (380×125 mm), 'Christ as the Gardener' (380×125 mm), and the 'Resurrection', are apparently by the same sculptor. The fragment showing the 'Taking down from The Cross' (317×265 mm) was made in the Netherlands. All five are from a retable or retables depicting the Passion Story.

PSAS, lxii (1927–8), 219–22

F20   Crosier of oak

Scotland Early 15th century
270×105 mm
Found in 1848 in a tomb in the north side of the presbytery of the Cathedral, Kirkwall, thought to have been that of Bishop Thomas Tulloch (1422–55).
Edinburgh National Museum KJ 61

The wooden crozier which was found with an imitation chalice and paten both made of wax is likely to be a funerary model itself. It may be carved in imitation of a crozier belonging to the See.

PSAS, lix (1924–5), 244

F19   Five fragments of wooden altar retables

F19   Five fragments of wooden altar retables

F20 Crosier of oak

F22 Brass lectern

Low Countries or Scotland Early 16th century
1.68 m high, diam of base 0.55 m
Presented to the parish church of St Stephens, St Albans, by Sir Richard Lee of Sopwell who is thought to have acquired it in Edinburgh during the invasion of the English Army in 1544 under the Earl of Hertford.
St Albans, Parish Church of St Stephens

shoulder is an inscription which reads, SANCTE EGIDIE ORA PRO NOBIS ANNO DNI M CCC LXXXX V (Saint Giles pray for us, in the year of our Lord 1495)

Saint Giles was the patron saint of blacksmiths and a number of British pre-Reformation bells are dedicated to him. Below the inscription band is the sign 'xt' which is the founder's mark. The same mark has been found on a bell at Linlithgow, one at Uphall and also on a cooking pot, the so-called 'Soulis Pot', at Drumlanrig Castle, Dumfriesshire.

At the top of the bell, the argent is cracked and two of the original four canons have broken off. The number of canons is unusually few for a bell of this type, which would normally have six.

PSAS, xlvii (1912–13), 68–71; *Ayr Colls* (1947–9), 222

A brass eagle lectern with a wide spread base formerly supported on three feet, possibly resembling lions' paws. The claws of the birds' feet which may have been silver are missing. An inscription on the upper wave moulding of the central band on the stem reads: GEORGIUS CREICHTOUN EPISCOPUS DUNKELDENSIS, before which is a lion rampant on a plain shield. On the front and back of the globe above is an engraving of a bishop's mitre with a crozier in pale behind it. On the sides is a large shield with a lion rampant which represents the arms of the Crichton family.

The lectern is thought to have been made as a present from George Crichton, Bishop of Dunkeld, 1524–43, to Holyrood Abbey where he had previously been Abbot. It is likely to have been stolen from the Abbey by Sir Richard Lee, one of the Earl of Hertford's men who ransacked the building in 1544.

A few Medieval brass eagle lecterns survive in churches in Britain. Many of them are likely to have been imported from Flanders from where other brass items such as candelabra and tableware came into the country.

PSAS, xiii (1878–9), 287–94

F23 Brass chandelier

Low Countries 15th century
Formerly hung at the Skinners Altar in St John's Church, Perth. Now in the north transept.
St John's Church, Perth

The chandelier is a fine example of a type of multiple branch candelabra, incorporating a devotional image, which were imported into Britain from Flanders in great numbers in the fifteenth and sixteenth centuries. This one has twelve branches fashioned to resemble vine stems supporting the sconces, and at the top a statuette of the 'Beata Maria in Sole'—Our Lady in the Sun—a popular image in Europe in the period, inspired by a verse in Revelation, Chapter 12 where the Madonna is described as 'clothed with the sun and having the moon under her feet and stars about her head'.

The vast majority of such chandeliers were destroyed or lost during the Reformation but a few survive, for example in Berkley chapel, Bristol Cathedral and at St John's Church, Timberhill, Norwich. The Perth chandelier is the only surviving example in Scotland but St Nicholas Church, Aberdeen is known to have had four until the beginning of the nineteenth century. One of these incorporated a figure of St John the Baptist.

F24 Bronze pricket candlestick

France, Limoges *c.* 1100
Found during digging in the foundations of the Parish Church of Kinnoull near Perth.
Edinburgh, National Museum KJ 22

The candlestick was originally decorated with champlevé enamel which has eroded leaving only traces of blue enamel around the designs in the metal. A decoration of roundels flanked by wyverns can be seen on the tripod base of the candlestick while the knop and the tray are decorated with bands of foliaceous ornament. One of the legs has been replaced recently. This is a typical example of a candle-stick produced in Limoges in the twelfth and thirteenth centuries and used widely throughout Europe.

PSAS, iii (1857–60), 339

F25 Bronze censer

Scotland 13th century
150 × 100 mm
Found under the floor of the old church at Garvock, Kincardineshire.
Edinburgh, National Museum KJ 26

The cast bronze censer consists of a bowl with a foot and a domed, stepped cover decorated with a series of keyhole and quatrefoil shaped perforations and engraved ring and dot motifs.

F23 Brass chandelier

F25 Bronze censer

It has been suspended on four chains which originally passed through the coupled loops on the bowl and cover. The bottom of the censer has been burnt out through frequent use and has been repaired with a patch of bronze.

PSAS, xxi (1886–7), 180–82

F26 Silver chalice and paten

Scotland 13th century
From the grave of a bishop excavated at Whithorn Priory near Wigtown, Galloway, which also contained a crozier, and a large multiple gem ring.
Edinburgh, National Museum

The paten is made of silver-gilt, shaped by two depressions now somewhat flattened out. Inside the inner quatrefoil depression is an engraving of the 'Manus Dei' (Hand of God, making the sign of the blessing) framed by engraved circles enclosing a wavy line. The design is usual among patens of the thirteenth century. A similar example was found in the tomb of Archbishop Walter de Gray (d. 1255) in York Cathedral.

The chalice consists of an undecorated silver bowl to which is fixed a long, broken-off silver tang. The original silver stem of the chalice seems to have been

taken off before it was placed in the burial and a wooden one, of which fragments remain, put in its place for economic reasons.

F27 The Fetternear banner

Scotland Early 16th century
1.56×0.79 m
Given by the Leslies of Balquhain, who inherited the barony of Fetternear in the sixteenth century, to the Catholic Church of Our Lady of the Garioch and St John in Aberdeen, built in 1859.
Edinburgh, National Museum LF 23

The banner is the only known ecclesiastical banner surviving from pre-Reformation times. It is made of a single piece of linen, recently adapted at the top to accommodate a modern wooden baton, embroidered in the centre with the 'Image of Pity' showing the figure of Christ with wounds surrounded by the Instruments of the passion; below

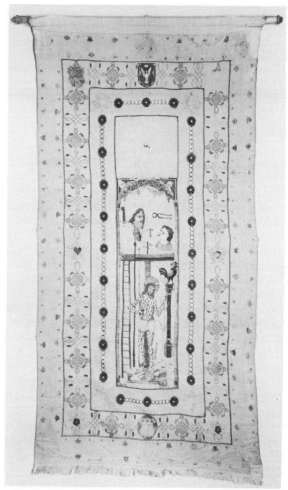

F27 The Fetternear banner

F26   Silver chalice and paten

Him the open sepulchre, the seamless robe and the three dice. Above the T-shaped cross are the heads of Judas and a mocking Jew. The panel is framed by a rosary with white beads separated by red rose medallions. The intermediate border is embroidered with interlinked cordeliers symbolising the unity of a pious brotherhood, interrupted along the top with coats of arms of which two are clear; in the left hand corner—the arms of Gavin Douglas Bishop of Dunkeld and provost of St Giles, Edinburgh 1503–21, and a fanciful coat of arms of the Holy Ghost. At the bottom is the coat of arms of Graham of Fintry. The outermost border is unfinished, but consists of a design made up of two motifs, the columbine and the scallop shell.

The colours of the silks have remained remarkably true perhaps due to the fact that the banner has been kept rolled up for most of its life.

The themes of the embroidered decoration suggest that the banner was probably made for the confraternity of the Holy Blood attached to St Giles, a group which included merchants, nobles and even King James IV. Gavin Douglas, Bishop of Dunkeld,

was provost of St Giles for a number of years. Graham of Fintry may be identified with Alexander Graham, one of the four kirkmasters of the Confraternity who was probably responsible for the commissioning of the banner.

The unfinished state of the banner has been ascribed to Douglas's flight to England in 1521 or his death in 1522. It may never have been used.

Innes Rev, vii (1956), 69–86

F28   **Portrait of William Elphinstone** (1431–1514)

Low Countries
University of Aberdeen

William Elphinstone was a bishop of the See of Aberdeen and the founder of Aberdeen University. His portrait is one of the earliest surviving paintings with a Scottish provenance. It may have formed part of a large polyptych altar piece like the Trinity Church Altarpiece in the National Gallery of Scotland.

F29 Chalice veil

Scotland 16th century
457×381 mm
The veil has been attached as a cover to a copy of a charter of 1322 by Robert Bruce to the Abbey of Arbroath, (86c), which was one of several documents in the Charter Chest of Arbroath Abbey inherited by the Maule family of Panmure House, Angus.
Scottish Record Office

An embroidered linen Chalice veil in the corners of which are small scrolls with four words IESUS EST AMOR MEUS (Jesus is my love) in Gothic minuscule characters. In the centre is embroidered a simplified representation of a eucharistic shrine consisting of a monstrance with branched candlesticks. The design reflects the popular devotion to the Holy Eucharist in Scotland in pre-Reformation times.

Innes Rev, xv (1964), 109–11

SELECT BIBLIOGRAPHY

T. K. Abbot *A Catalogue of Manuscripts in the Library of Trinity College, Dublin* (Dublin, 1900).
R. B. Armstrong *The Irish and Highland Harps* (Edinburgh, 1904).
J. Beckwith *Ivory Carvings in Early Medieval England* (London, 1972).
T. S. R. Boase *English Art 1100–1216* (Oxford, 1953).
C. R. Borland *Descriptive Catalogue of the Western Medieval Manuscripts in Edinburgh University Library* (Edinburgh, 1916).
A. H. Constable *The Kennet Ciborium* (Edinburgh, 1890).
G. R. C. Davis *Medieval Cartularies of Great Britain* (London, 1958).
A. Goldschmidt *Die Elfenbeinskulpturen*, vol. 4 (Berlin, 1926).
R. K. Hannay *Rentale Dunkeldense* (Scot. Hist. Soc., 1915).
E. Hawkins *Medallic Illustrations of the History of Great Britain* 2 vols (London, 1885).
M. R. James *A Descriptive Catalogue of the Manuscripts in the Library of Corpus Christi College* (Cambridge, 1912). *A Descriptive Catalogue of the Manuscripts in St John's College* (Cambridge, 1913). *A Catalogue of the Medieval Manuscripts in the University Library, Aberdeen* (Aberdeen, 1932).
N.R. Ker *Medieval Libraries of Great Britain* (2nd edition, London, 1964). *Medieval Manuscripts in British Libraries*, vol 1 (Oxford, 1969); vol 2 (London, 1977).
D. McRoberts *Catalogue of Scottish Medieval Liturgical Books and Fragments* (Glasgow, 1953).
W. S. Mitchell *A History of Scottish Bookbinding* (Aberdeen 1955).
F. Macken & H. H. E. Craster *A Summary Catalogue of Western Manuscripts in the Bodleian Library* (Oxford, 1937).
C. Oman *British Rings* (London, 1974).
PSAS Proceedings of the Society of Antiquaries of Scotland (1851–   ).
J. S. Richardson *The Mediaeval Stone Carver in Scotland* (Edinburgh, 1964).

– & H. B. MacIntosh *Elgin Cathedral* (HMSO, 1950).
M. Rickert *Painting in Britain: The Middle Ages* (Harmondsworth, 1954).
K. A. Steer & J. W. M. Bannerman *Late Medieval Monumental Sculpture in the West Highlands* (Edinburgh, 1977).
J. H. Stevenson & M. Wood *Scottish Heraldic Seals*, 3 vols (Glasgow, 1940).
M. Taylor *The Lewis Chessmen* (London, 1978).
A. B. Tonnochy *Catalogue of British Seal-Dies in the British Museum* (London, 1952).
F. Werner & J. P. Gibson *Catalogue of Western Manuscripts in the Old Royal and King's Collections* (London, 1921).
J. Young & P. H. Aitken *A Catalogue of the Manuscripts in the Hunterian Museum in the University of Glasgow* (Glasgow, 1908).